Beans, Bullets & Canapés

Feeding a Fighter Pilot
And a
Few Other Boys and Girls

By

Marti Giacobe

Marti Giacobe

Warning—Disclaimer

The authors and publishers have produced this book with the understanding that readers are already familiar with most basic and some advanced cooking and food preparation techniques, and that they exercise basic sanitary procedures in the kitchen. Cooking times are approximate and all prepared foods that require minimum safe cooking temperatures should always be checked with a reliable thermometer. Every effort has been made to make this book as complete and as accurate as possible. However, there may be mistakes, both typographical and in content.

First Printing 2004

ISBN 0-9758936-0-2

Manufactured in the United States by Vaughan Printing, Inc.

Dedication

Twenty-six years, 3 months, 18 days, 7 hours and 52 minutes in uniform. But nobody's counting. Seventeen assignments, eighteen moves, four cats, two kids, no birds or fish, and a lot of friends later, we began calling Marietta, Georgia home (6½ miles due west of the Big Chicken to be precise). It's also kind of scary. We never had to paint walls before, we just packed up everything we had and moved across country to a different house!

But everywhere we went, we had to eat, so this is more of a cookbook than it is a travelogue. Spending over a quarter century traveling the world, we just HAD to include some stories for you to enjoy. While many of these are rib tickling, none are intended to criticize the most powerful Air Force in the world, or the proud men and women who continue to serve. To the contrary, we hope to praise them in the highest regard, for we've been there and know what it takes. "Been there. Done that. Got the T-shirt!"

Throughout our travels around the world, we were always intent on building traditions that solidified our family life wherever we were stationed. Thanksgiving dinner always included that special turkey dressing that everyone looked forward to. New Year's Day brunch always included a Shrimp Creole casserole, and Easter Leg of Lamb isn't complete without mint jelly (often homemade).

Our travels to distant lands also gave us the opportunity to try new foods and challenge ourselves to duplicate them in our own kitchen. Our many successes were often punctuated with memorable disasters, but perseverance and return visits often did the trick.

So, simply put, this work is dedicated to the people in our lives who have inspired us the most: our family and close friends who have helped along the way, put up with our challenges, and encouraged us throughout. We love you all.

Tony & Marti Giacobe

HOTLINKS

The CD-ROM version of this cookbook has hotlinks throughout, allowing you to click on a Table of Contents entry and jump directly to that section or recipe.
Additionally, there are several MPEG video clips and a ton of pictures hyperlinked from the recipes.   Click on the underlined hotlink to view these. All MPEGs function normally with Windows Media Player 8.0, and all pictures are JPEGs.

A portion of the proceeds of this book benefit various Atlanta based charities.

For additional copies, visit us online at www.giacobe.net or www.beansbullets.com ,
send us an email at cookbook@giacobe.net
Or use the Order Form on last page

Before We Begin

Whether a good cook comes from a hereditary line of culinary masters or learns from a specific environment, I believe that I was destined to be at least a passable cook. As a child I listened to radio cooking shows with my mother. Then with the magic of television at the age of five, I was transported to Chicago and the "Francois Pope School of Cooking." Right after my daily disappointment of not being seen in Miss Frances's mirror on Ding Dong School, I watched the creation of beautifully crafted food. The chefs wore gleaming white coats and had every ingredient pre-measured into a little dish. My love of china and crystal as well as a man in a crisp uniform could have begun here.

As for coming from a long line of cooks, that is true as well. Tony's father came from a farming family from the hills just outside of Rome Italy, near San Marcos in the province of Foggia. Their home was a simple one, with a pot on the fire almost constantly. When Grandma Giacobbe came to this country in the early 1900s, she brought along all of her favorite recipes, many which Tony & I still use today with only minor modifications.

My ancestors were also engaged in farming. The family homestead and dairy farm was in north central Illinois. Whether dinner was a beef roast or a rabbit pie, vegetables from the garden always accompanied dinner. Wherever we set up housekeeping, we also established a little garden area. Today we concentrate on herbs. My Grandma Emling could feed a crew of farm hands with ease. On the French side, my Grandma Seroy only made pots of soup large enough for an army. There was always room at the table for another person. Whether it was my French grandmother's garlic laced pork roast or my German grandmother's velvety yeast rolls, I learned at an early age to discern flavors and textures. This appreciation for the arts and crafts of the kitchen started my love of food and cooking.

I was amazed that not all kids could fry a chicken over an open fire and make gravy by the age of ten, or serve-up a whole Thanksgiving Dinner at twelve. Those were things I just did. I must admit, that I never learned how to throw a ball well or run a 50-yard dash.

My biggest inspirations in cooking came with marriage to Tony, raising our family of Nick and Drew, and the military "Road Show." Commencing in Enid, Oklahoma in 1973 to the Great Wall of China and back to the USA, I observed, I tasted and I cooked, recreating many of the dishes I found. I may not be able to carry a tune, but my taste buds have helped me master the complex seasonings of Asia as well as the delicate pastries of Europe.

As world travelers and now as real estate professionals, we've come to appreciate a love of the land with family traditions and hope to pass on a sense of tradition in the foods we create. As you read through the following pages, I hope that you enjoy the trip and get at least a couple of smiles from the stories. Then you may take a recipe or two and try them, expand on them and make them your own. After all of that is accomplished, share your love of creating food with your friends and family.

Marti

Table Of Contents

7

I. Appetizers

Graduation and commissioning at Officers Training School (OTS) started us on the great journey that we affectionately call "The Road Show". Over the course of the Air Force career, we moved often, just like everybody else in the military. That was the price we paid for flying those high performance, sleek, snazzy jets.

We had 18 moves in 27 years, and we're counting only those places where we actually lived and received mail and our kids enrolled in the schools. State-side, we lived on-base only once, at Fort Riley, and overseas both times in Korea. At all the other places, we bought a house: seven to be exact, so we're very much in tune with the upheaval that moving brings to a family and maybe explains why we're in Real Estate today.

After Tony graduated from OTS at Lackland AFB in San Antonio Texas, we made our first government move to Vance AFB, Oklahoma for student pilot training. We rented one side of a duplex on the east side of Enid. The year moved quickly, dominated by the Undergraduate Pilot Training program, its functions and group activities, many of them were a "bring a dish" of one kind or another. Most were so thoroughly organized that dishes were assigned by category just out of the need for taking care of about 20 families and bachelors. Of course there were always the class or section party which included a truly interesting variety of foods. At one party that went really late, we ran out of snacks, so the host featured a "mystery snack" which had very

mixed reviews. Seems his "mystery snack" wasn't any mystery to his dog: it was a dish of dry dog food.

In the pilot training class we had a lot of National Guard guys, several Iranian air cadets, and two Norwegian trainees, which tended to keep things interesting. The Iranians were very prone to airsickness, and many times throughout the week the flying squadron loudspeakers would page one of them to go clean up his airplane after a flight.

The year-long pilot training program culminated with graduation and awarding wings on 25 July 1974, and we moved across town into our first new house. Tony's schedule as a T-37 Instructor Pilot was set by the flying needs of the student pilot classes he had. He spent the tour in F flight, working his way up from line instructor to flight standards evaluation officer, training students from nine classes in all during our tour there, usually "owning" about three students per class. He turned out to be a rather gifted instructor evidenced by the fact that the flight commander always presented him with the challenges of "not-so gifted" students who were having a hard time. Most challenging were the Ethiopians in one class, when he had to rely on his high school French a couple times in order to be effective.

Life was very predictable and cooking meals was easy to orchestrate because of the structured duty day, making the "When's Dinner" question easy to solve. Here was the time that we could put together entire menus and it would all be ready at the same time. We kept a schedule for dinner at 5:30 for the boys. If Tony was home, he ate with us. If not, he ate a warmed plate. If I was unhappy with him, I put the salad on the plate in the oven. Luckily, we purchased our first microwave oven in 1975 and Tony's dinner wasn't stuck to the plate on late weeks. No matter when we ate, we always had an appetizer on hand like the home-made smokey salami rolls, or cheeseball and crackers.

Whether truly an appetizer, an adjunct to a meal, something for guests to munch on while they mingle, a dish that easily becomes a full course, or even a complete meal (like the Calamari below), "finger foods" have their place for all occasions. Most notable, fun, and most complicated in preparation are the Yaki Mandu, or Korean "potstickers" toward the end of this chapter. Most cultures have their own unique version. When we were in Korea the first time, our housekeeper taught us how to make these. Tony videotaped the entire session, and then when we wanted to include it here, he thought that the tape had been recycled long ago, so we reconstructed the recipe from 15-year-old memories. Then, two weeks later, he found the tape, and we just HAD to watch it. We had successfully gotten the recipe very close to the original!

Calamari

Calamari is a wonderful delicacy, but there are pitfalls. Cook it too long and it comes out like rubber. If they are too large, they'll be tough. Too small and it's a lifetime until you finish cleaning them. Doc and Doris (Tony's parents) used to buy them in Pensacola and tell the grocer they were using them for bait, then go home and cook them, because they were a buck cheaper that way. You find these most often breaded and deep fried, but Tony's cousins like them cooked this way, and they do come out tender and sweet.

2-3 pounds Calamari, cleaned and cut into pieces
Olive oil
2-3 onions
1 teaspoon salt

Put about a half inch of oil in the bottom of a 3 quart sauce pan. Quarter the onions into 8ths or thinner, resulting in large slices. Throw the onions and calamari into the sauce pan. Add salt. Stir to mix, then bring to boil covered, or until the foam bubbles to the top. Serve immediately.

Cheese Ball

Most purchased cheese balls are much too large. They are made to last a whole season and not the get-together of a few friends for a glass of wine. I make cheese balls about the size of a small apple. They can also be made into logs of nearly any length or diameter depending on the size of the group partaking. I make up a lot of these in different sizes in October or November to take us through the holiday season. Any cheese ball can be adjusted to a more usable size. Double wrap and freeze until needed.

16 ounces cream cheese
6 ounces cheddar cheese
4 ounces Swiss cheese
1 ounce parmesan cheese
¼ Cup minced dry onions
1 teaspoon garlic powder
¼ Cup dried parsley
2 teaspoons Worcestershire
½ Cup evaporated milk

For decorating
Paprika
Whole cloves
Small bay leaves
Chopped nuts
Dry chopped parsley

Beat cream cheese until fluffy. Stir in shredded cheddar, Swiss and Parmesan, dried onions, garlic powder, Worcestershire sauce and parsley. Add evaporated milk until the mixture makes a very thick paste. It will be lumpy. Let rest. The dry ingredients will absorb the milk. The onions and bits of the firmer cheeses will be evident.

Make a ball the size that you would serve as an appetizer with crackers. I usually start with a ball the size of a large lemon or a small apple. Roll in paprika. Make a dent in the top with your knuckle. Place a whole clove upside down in the dent with a small bay leaf. Wow! It's a little apple. Refrigerate until firm. Make other balls and roll in chopped nuts. Or roll a log shape in chopped nuts. Make cheese balls until you run out of mixture. Or make very small balls the size of a walnut. That's perfect for one person.

Chopped Chicken Liver Pate

My mother grew-up in a neighborhood of either first generation Americans or Americans who just stepped off the boat at Ellis Island. She told me that you didn't need to see to know where you were in the neighborhood. A good sniff of the aromas that drifted from each kitchen would tell you whose home you were approaching. This recipe started in Kankakee, Illinois and was developed along the way. My friend Hank said a hard boiled egg added to my recipe would really improve my chopped liver. Thanks Hank, it did.

1 pound chicken livers
1 small onion, minced
1 stalk celery chopped
Salt and pepper
2 hard cooked eggs
1 teaspoon Worcestershire sauce
½ Cup Miracle Whip

Place livers, onion, and celery in a heavy saucepan. Cover with water. Bring to a boil, reduce to simmer and cook covered until the livers are tender. Drain and cool.

Process the livers in a food processor until a smooth past forms. In a medium bowl season livers with the Worcestershire Sauce, salt and pepper. Moisten with the Miracle Whip. Start with 3 tablespoons, adding up to ½ cup as needed, to achieve a light, loose consistency. Press the peeled hard cooked eggs through a coarse sieve into the chicken livers. Adjust the moisture and seasoning.

Serve well chilled. Decorate with sliced green olives and pimentos. Serve with crackers and thin slice rye bread rounds.

Cocktail Shrimp with Sauce

1 pound medium or large shrimp
1 can of beer
2 Tablespoons whole mustard seeds
1 Tablespoon chopped fresh garlic
1 Tablespoon minced dried parsley
½ teaspoon celery seeds
1 large green bay leaf
1 small dried red pepper or ½ teaspoon pepper flakes

Clean and remove the veins from the shrimp. If you're cooking a lot or the atmosphere is very informal, leave the shells on. With a larger crowd it slows the consumption to leave the shelling to the guests. Always leave on the tails. It makes a nicer presentation and gives a little handle for dipping. Set aside and keep refrigerated. In a 2 quart or 3 quart saucepan, bring the beer and seasoning to a boil. Reduce to a simmer and simmer at least 10 minutes. Return to the boil. If the liquid has reduced too much either add another beer or water. The beer will foam so watch carefully to avoid a mess. Add shrimp to the pan. They cook very quickly, just a minute or two is all it takes. Stir lightly to get all shrimp cooked at the same time. When they are pink and no longer translucent they are done. Drain and chill over a bowl of ice or in iced water immediately. For shrimp cocktail, chill the shrimps thoroughly.

For a formal shrimp cocktail, assemble as follows: In an American champagne glass fill the bottom with shredded iceberg lettuce. Hang 4 large or 6 medium shrimps on the edge of the glass with the tails toward the outside. Spoon chilled cocktail sauce (next page) in the center on top of the lettuce. Add a lemon wedge to the service plate.

Cocktail Sauce

½ Cup ketchup
1 teaspoon Worcestershire Sauce
Juice of half a lemon
A few drops of hot sauce
1 to 2 Tablespoons horseradish

Crab Stuffed Mushrooms

Our friend Vince taught me to clean blue crab. There's not a great deal of meat in each crab. To get enough meat for one crab cake, it will take 2 or 3 crabs. That's why those things are so expensive. These mushrooms are great for a cocktail buffet and it doesn't take quite as much crab meat as a crab cake.

2 pounds fresh mushrooms
1 pound crab meat
½ teaspoon garlic powder
1 small onion finely minced
¼ teaspoon dry mustard
½ teaspoon each dry thyme, marjoram, parsley
A pinch of cayenne pepper
3 Tablespoons to ½ Cup Miracle Whip
Paprika

Clean the mushroom by rubbing the dust off the caps with a mushroom brush or dry towel. Remove stems and use to for another purpose. Place cap with stem side up on broiler proof pan. Mix crab meat, seasoning and moisten with Miracle Whip (start with 3 tablespoons and add more until you achieve a light, loose consistency). Mound a teaspoon or more of crab mixture into the cap. Sprinkle with paprika.

At this point the mushroom can be refrigerated for a few hours or up to one day. Just before serving, place under the broiler and broil until the crab mixture bubbles. Serve at once.

Crustini or "Brochetta"

1/3 Cup minced red onion or shallot
1/3 Cup basil in a chiffonade (or 2 basil cubes - see Chapter 6)
2 cloves finely minced garlic
2 Tablespoons olive oil
6 plum tomatoes chopped into ½ inch dice
2 Tablespoons wine vinegar
Salt & fresh cracked black pepper

Mix all ingredients together and let marinate for at least 1 hour. Serve spoonfuls on toasted rustic style Italian bread, sliced very thinly or thick if you prefer. In the winter use 2 basil cubes.

Deviled Eggs

1 dozen hard cooked eggs
1 teaspoon Worchester Sauce
1 teaspoon salad mustard
½ teaspoon salt
½ Cup Miracle Whip
Paprika

Peel eggs and cut lengthwise. Pop yolk out. Do not break white. Mash yolk. Using electric mixer add other ingredients except paprika. Spoon or pipe filling into whites. Sprinkle with paprika. Chill until ready to use. These eggs will not keep more than a day.

Garlic Bread

Slice a loaf of Italian or French bread
¼ pound margarine or butter
2 teaspoons garlic powder

Slice the bread in 1 inch thick pieces, but leave the slices connected at the bottom crust. Whip the butter and garlic with electric mixer. Spread on each side of the slices of bread. Wrap loaf in aluminum foil. Bake at 350 degrees for 10-15 minutes.

Parmesan Cheese Toast

The first restaurant where I worked used this toast as the bed for a small steak and called it a sandwich. It's a good idea or use the toast for a side dish with soup or with a salad for a lighter meal.

1 inch thick slices of Italian or French bread
¼ pound melted butter
½ - ¾ Cup Parmesan cheese

Dip the bread in the melted butter, then dip into cheese, then grill or pan fry on both sides.

Cucumber Sandwiches

This recipe earned a passing grade with my very European friend Morag. Of course I was not sure that she wasn't just starved. Give them a try the next time the cucumbers look great at the market.

1 cucumber
Firm white bread - Pepperidge Farm is good
Softened butter
Softened cream cheese
Dill weed

Try to use a cucumber that has not been waxed. Then you can eat the skin. Select a cucumber that is firm and has few or very small seeds. Cut the bread with a canapé cutter, a small wine glass or even in squares with a knife. The bread pieces should be about the size of the diameter of the cucumber. Butter lightly. Spread with a bit of cream cheese. Either peel or score cucumber with a knife to decorate the edge. Top the prepared bread with a quarter inch thick slice of cucumber. Sprinkle with fresh or dried dill weed. Serve at once or within an hour of completion.

Gougere Aux Fine Herbes

If you've had one too many chip and dip nibbles at a cocktail buffet, this will be a treat. It's quick to assemble and can be baked as people begin to arrive. It can also be baked at home and cut into wedges to take to a party. I've never had any leftovers of this dish.

½ Cup (1 stick) butter
1 Cup water
1 Cup all purpose flour
4 eggs
1 teaspoon dried mustard
½ teaspoon thyme
½ teaspoon oregano
1 teaspoon chervil
2 Tablespoon chopped parsley
½ teaspoon basil
1 teaspoon salt
¼ teaspoon cayenne
1 ½ Cup grated Swiss cheese

Cut the butter into pieces, place in saucepan with water and bring to boil. When butter is melted remove pan from heat and add all the flour. Beat vigorously until smooth paste forms, return to medium heat and beat until paste is shiny, about 1 minute. Remove from heat. Make a well in paste, break 1 egg into the well and beat vigorously until thoroughly blended; add the remaining 3 eggs, 1 egg at a time. Beat in mustard, thyme, oregano, chervil, parsley, basil salt and cayenne. Fold in grated cheese.

Preheat oven to 450 degrees. Lightly grease large baking sheet, 11x18x1. Sprinkle lightly with flour. With a fingertip, using a round 7-inch cake pan as a guide, trace two 7-inch circles in flour. Drop cheese-egg mixture by tablespoons onto the circles to form 2 rings. Smooth each ring with rubber spatula. Place in oven and bake 12 minutes, turn oven down to 325 degrees and bake additional 30 minutes. Remove from oven. Serve hot or cold, breaking into chunks or cutting into wedges.

Hog's Snot
(or Chili Con Queso)

This version of Chili Con Queso got its beginnings when Tony was flying the A-10, affectionately known as the "Warthog". Somehow we got assigned several times together with "Wild Bill", another A-10 pilot who was often rather boisterous and entertaining. I think it was at Tucson that we adopted a liking for the southwestern fare, and we always needed something to wash the beer down with. I created this tidbit as a great dip or appetizer, and since we were all flying "hogs" at the time, it became "hog's snot", so very appropriate for the guys flying these machines around the world.

When I worked in radio in Austin, Texas, the sales manager and sales people would occasionally go out to lunch together to a hole in the wall Mexican restaurant on Guadaloupe Ave. We'd all order the same thing, which was the "Perkin's Special." This isn't exactly their recipe, however it can be reproduced almost everywhere, and makes a great hot dip for chips.

1 pound ground beef
1 can diced tomatoes
1 pound Velveeta
1-4 Jalapeno peppers
¼ to ½ Cup bell pepper

Brown the ground beef, leaving some chunks. Dice the peppers into a fine dice, removing seeds. Stir peppers, tomatoes and Velveeta into the drained ground beef. Melt over medium heat, stirring often. This will thicken as it cools. If it seems too thick, add a little tomato juice or beer. Serve with tortilla chips or spoon over tortilla chips layered with shredded lettuce and diced tomatoes to make a "Perkins Special" (add picante sauce over the top).

Stuffed Grape Leaves with Egg-Lemon Sauce

1 8-ounce jar grape leaves
Filling:
½ Cup raw long grain rice
1 Tablespoon olive oil
½ Cup chopped yellow onions
2 Tablespoons chopped fresh Italian parsley
½ teaspoon dried dill weed
Juice of ½ lemon
½ pound lean lamb, coarsely ground or chopped
½ teaspoon allspice
2 cloves garlic crushed
Salt & pepper to taste
Broth:
1 Cup chicken stock or canned chicken broth
Juice of ½ lemon
Sauce:
1 batch Egg Lemon Sauce

Mix all the ingredients for the filling. Pick out the smallest leaves in the jar and set aside. Use some of these leaves to place a single layer in the bottom of the pot.

Cut the stems off the grape leaves. Spread a leaf on the counter, bottom side up, stem toward you. Place 1 teaspoon of the filling in the center of the leaf. Fold the stem end over the filling, then fold the sides over to secure the filing, then roll from you toward the tip of the leaf, forming a small cigar or cylinder. The size should be approximately 2 ½ inches long and ¾ inch wide. Do not wrap these too tightly as the rice needs room for expansion when it cooks.

Using a 2 quart heavy lidded kettle, place the rolled up leaves on top of the single layer in the bottom. Place the rolls up against each other rather tightly so that they will not come undone while cooking. Cover them with a layer of unrolled leaves, and then add another layer of rolled leaves. Continue until all rolled leaves are in the pot. Top with the remaining unrolled leaves.

Place a medium plate over the top of the leaves, as a weight. Mix the chicken stock and lemon juice for the broth, and pour over the leaves in the pot. Cover and bring to a light simmer. Cook 1 hour. Remove the pan from the heat and allow it to cool for 1 more hour. Do not remove the lid or the leaves will darken. Serve warm with Egg Lemon Sauce on top.

Egg Lemon Sauce (Avgolemono)

½ Cup lamb stock or chicken stock
1 egg
Juice of ½ lemon
1 Tablespoon water
Salt & pepper to taste
Roux:
1 Tablespoon butter and 1 Tablespoon flour, cooked (Chapter 6)

Heat the stock and prepare the roux. Thicken the stock with the roux. In a separate bowl whip the eggs, lemon juice, and water together until frothy. Add the eggs to the thickened stock, stirring constantly. Bring to temperature but do not boil, stirring all the time until thick. Salt and pepper.

Blue Cheese Spread

Spread this on crisp apples or pears. The spread is also very good with savory crackers. It can be frozen in portions for later use.

2 ounces Blue cheese
1 8-ounce package cream cheese
¼ pound butter

Soften butter and cream cheese to room temperature. Mix together well with electric mixer or by hand. Stir in blue cheese. Chill until firm.

Salmon Spread

This is a great little canapé or starter and is nice to make up when houseguests will be with you for several days. Keep in an airtight container. It should hold up for about a week in the refrigerator. The basic recipe came from Fairbanks, Alaska using smoked salmon. Since smoked salmon is a little hard to find sometimes in "The Lower 48", I adapted it to use regular canned salmon.

4 ounces of regular cream cheese
8 ounces red salmon, canned
1 teaspoon liquid smoke
1 Tablespoon lemon juice

Beat cream cheese with a hand mixer until fluffy. Drain the salmon. Add to the cream cheese along with the liquid smoke and lemon juice. Beat, leaving as much texture as possible. Include the bones; this adds a little more calcium. Besides you paid for the whole can of salmon, use it. Chill before serving. Spread on crackers, thin slices of party rye bread or use thin crackers as dippers.

Yaki Mandu

I have made thousands of these little pies filled with meat, onion, carrots, Tofu, rice noodles and of course garlic. They take a very long time if you make the skins from scratch. I have only done this with our Korean housekeeper. Use the round wonton skins for a very good substitute. The skins should have little blisters on them when they are fried to a light golden brown. We have even gotten another generation of Giacobes on the road to Korean dining. Grandson Stephen loves Yaki Mandu and will eat rice with a bit of Kalbi (Chapter 3).

100 round Wonton skins (from a store carrying Asian products)
2 ounces Chinese bean thread noodles
1/3 pound ground beef
½ Cup shredded carrots
½ Cup minced onion
4 ounces diced water chestnuts
4 ounces firm tofu
1 Tablespoon minced ginger root
2 Tablespoons minced garlic
1 teaspoon MSG
1 package Shitake mushroom
1/3 Cup snipped chives
1 Tablespoon rice wine vinegar
1 to 2 Tablespoons soy sauce
1 teaspoon sesame oil

Bring to a boil enough water to cook the rice noodles. Cook drain and rinse. Set aside. In a large sauté pan brown ground beef. Stir-fry with a little oil the beef, carrots, onion, chives, and water chestnuts. Stir in the garlic, MSG, ginger root and finely sliced Shitake mushroom. Chop the rice noodles into one-inch long pieces. Stir noodles, rice wine, soy sauce and sesame oil into the pan. Wipe edge of skin with water, place 1 teaspoon filling in the center, fold over, seal, and crimp with a fork. Place on a baking sheet that has been sprayed with vegetable spray. The half-moon pies should not touch. Fry and serve or freeze to firm uncovered. Transfer to a re-sealable plastic bag. Freeze until ready for use. Fry in deep fat at 350 to 375 degrees. Drain on absorbent paper. Dip in soy dipping sauce.

<u>Soy Dipping Sauce</u>

¼ Cup light soy sauce
1 Tablespoon rice vinegar
½ teaspoon toasted sesame seed
¼ teaspoon red pepper flakes (optional)

Stir together and place in a cupped dish for dipping.

Tortilla Cake

This makes a large amount. It's great to take to a party and looks a lot more difficult than it really is to make. The must-have here is a long, really sharp knife.

16 ounces cream cheese, softened
1 small can chopped black olives
1 small can chopped mild green chilies
About 16-20 flour tortillas 6 to 8 inches in diameter
Salsa or Picante Sauce

Using an electric mixer beat the cream cheese until fluffy. Add the olives and green chilies. On a footed cake plate or other serving plate spread about 2 teaspoons cream cheese mixture and cover with a tortilla. This will keep the "cake" from shifting while assembling. Spread each tortilla with cream cheese mixture edge to edge. Top with another until there are no more tortillas or no more cream cheese. Try to make the layers even. Don't worry if you have a couple of tortillas or a little cream cheese left. Chill covered with plastic wrap for at least 4 hours (over night is best). To serve, cut narrow wedges. You should get 16 or so from one "cake." This is where that really sharp, long bladed knife comes into play. Garnish with radish and tomato roses and shredded green onions if desired. Serve with the salsa or picante sauce in a side dish. Wedges are dipped in the salsa. Sometimes the wedges are pulled apart and dipped for more dainty appetites.

Smokey Salami Rolls

I am nearly certain that a pound of this sausage cemented my "A" in my final course in Public Relations at Kansas State. I wasn't taking any chances. The professor was a huge man who ate like there was no tomorrow. I dropped off the salami with the professor and ran a 10-minute errand. I stopped back to ask a question and he was finishing the last bite. You do what you have to do.

4 pounds lean ground beef
¼ Cup curing salt (Morton's Tender Quick)
2 Tablespoons Liquid Smoke
1½ teaspoons garlic powder
2 teaspoons coarse ground black pepper
½ Cup water

     The large table-top Kitchen Aid mixer does a beautiful job on this dish. Or you can do it by hand and get a great workout. Mix all ingredients well. I mix in the Kitchen Aid about 4 minutes. Shape into 4 rolls, wrap in plastic wrap, and chill for 24 hours. Place logs on broiler rack with water in the pan portion of the rack. Bake at 225 degrees for 4 hours. Turn ¼ turn once an hour.
     Keeps indefinitely in the freezer. Keeps weeks in the refrigerator. If using ground turkey, omit the water. The turkey meat is much softer and might slip through the rack a bit. Serve sliced thinly. It's great with mustard, cheeses and crackers.

Little Neck Clams

This is one of my favorites. They are a bit messy, but the flavor of the butter sauce soaked into a crusty French loaf is near perfection for a first course in a very casual setting. A few warm wet washcloths on hand are a very good idea.

2 pounds fresh Little Neck Clams
4 to 6 Tablespoons butter
1 Cup diced celery
1 Cup diced yellow onion
2 to 3 Tablespoons garlic
1 Cup white wine
Handful of fresh parsley
Loaf of crusty French bread

Make sure clams are clean and alive. Scrub the sand off the shells and rinse in clean water. Discard any clams that are open and will not close to gentle pressure. Set aside.

Sauté the vegetables (but not the parsley) in butter until translucent, but not brown. Add wine and reduce to fifty percent of volume. Place clams in pot in an even layer. I use a big sauté pan. Cover and let steam for 3 or 4 minutes. Check to see if all clams have opened. If most of the clams are still closed steam another minute or two. Remove any unopened clams. Dust with chopped parsley. Serve at once with ice cold white wine, warm crusty bread and those washcloths for wiping hands. Of course you must dip your bread in the sauce. Wash the shells and make something decorative out of them ala "Martha".

Cheeseball pg 18

Grape Leaves pg 26

Smokey Salami pg 30

Yaki Mandu pg 28

Chorizo pg 38

Eggs Benedict pg 35

French Toast pg 35

Migas pg 39

II. Breakfast

Just as breakfast foods begin our day, our assignment to Bergstrom AFB Texas was the beginning of our career in the "tactical fighter" world. Most pilots aspired to be fighter pilots, flying a "manly man's" machine and the competition for a fighter assignment was keen. When Tony got the news of our assignment to a KC-135 at Castle AFB in an air refueling unit, it was only a couple days later when the assignments officer called and asked if he would take an O-2 (Cessna 337 twin engine) to Bergstrom AFB in Texas instead.

The O-2 is not a fighter, but most pilots selected for an O-2 assignment would transition from the "Oscar Duck" into a fighter at the end of their assignment. He was so happy to get out of the Strategic Air Command assignment that he quickly said yes and asked how soon he had to report. When he told his boss what had happened, he congratulated him and then asked if he knew what an O-2 was. He admitted he didn't and then quickly found out. When he announced the happy news to me later that evening, I asked where Bergstrom was. Not knowing that either, he quickly made a few calls and happily found it nearby Austin, Texas. So our first real turning point in the career was done purely by someone else. We had jumped at the chance, not knowing the aircraft, mission, or even location of the new posting.

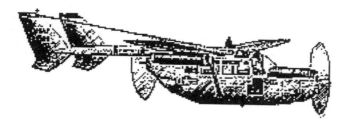

Flying the O-2 was a real kick and it was some of the best flying Tony did in his entire career. The plane was so small and so overloaded with equipment that a pilot had to really "feel" what

33

the aircraft was doing. It was easy to put the airplane into situations that could turn out to be disastrous because of the lack of power. In fact, just before we arrived, the unit had just had several aircraft accidents, killing five of the guys in three months.

One of the "nuances" of flying a little airplane like the O-2 was that by simply moving the seat back or forth, you could change the center of gravity of the airplane and cause it to climb or dive without touching any of the controls. They called it "sky surfing". It was safe and fun to do on long flights across the west Texas expanses. But one of our pilots got into a memorable situation when, during a long deployment leg somewhere east of El Paso, the seat lock opened, and his seat slid backwards. They always flew with two pilots in the airplane, so it would be an easy matter for the other pilot to take over – if only he could get his attention. Unable to reach the flight controls, he called out to him on what he thought was the intercom, and the problem was quickly solved. But not before the other six pilots in the flight, two Air Traffic Controllers, and about six commercial airliners on the same frequency heard his calls for help.

Austin, Texas was an outstanding town and we totally enjoyed the Texas cuisine. Barbeque took on new meaning and we frequently drove out of town for the best meals we ever had. Elgin sausage and country eateries with dance floors became the preferred haunts. Our assignments in the southwest introduced us to a cuisine that is now more "Americana" than anything else. Our favorites are the Migas, Chorizo, and Eg and Potato soft tacos. A lot of our desert southwest is punctuated with wonderful foods, including some interesting restaurant combinations. For example, it was difficult to find a main theme at the Chinese Mexican-American restaurant in Alamogordo, New Mexico.

Every culture has its own preference for the first meal of the day. The British fare is quite heavy, and often would fill you up for the entire day. Being on the continent meant that you feasted on prepared meats and cheeses. In the Far East, it was often fish-based with many institutions such as child care centers or schools *making fish soup (hot or cold). French Toast and Belgian Waffles can be considered "haute cuisine", and making your own isn't very time consuming or difficult.*

Eggs Benedict

4 English muffin halves, toasted
4 slices Canadian bacon
4 poached eggs
1 batch Hollandaise sauce (Chapter 6)

Toast the English muffins. Place on service plate. Add slice of warm Canadian bacon, and place a poached egg on it, and add a dab of hollandaise sauce (see Chapter 6). Serve warm with champagne or very dry white wine.

French Toast

2 eggs
1 Cup of milk
3 Tablespoons sugar
1 teaspoon vanilla
Leftover French or Italian bread cut into 1 inch thick slices

Beat eggs and sugar. Add milk and stir in vanilla. Soak bread in egg mixture. Leave long enough to absorb mixture without getting soggy. Grill or pan fry until evenly golden brown, turning as necessary. Keep in warming oven until all bread and mixture is used. Serve with applesauce and cinnamon instead of syrup.

Grilled Calves Liver with Buckwheat Pancakes

This was the first breakfast my parents introduced to my husband-to-be. Not being a big breakfast fan, Tony thought a good morning starter was 6 cookies and a bottle of cola. Tony now only rarely eats breakfast, and when he does it's after 10 a.m. and never this one. I would suggest this meal if you plan on chopping a cord of wood or hand turning a half acre garden. It will stick with you and give you plenty of energy to work like a horse. Make sure you add a couple of sunny side up eggs and a couple Cups of coffee. If you must, add a glass of juice.

1 pound sliced calves liver
All purpose flour
Salt and pepper
Vegetable oil
Buckwheat pancake mix

Dredge the liver in seasoned flour. Brown in vegetable oil quickly. Remove to a hold platter. Pour off excess oil. Return liver to the pan. Add a quarter of a cup of water to the pan and steam the liver until well done. A sauce will develop. Adjust season.

Make pancakes according to package directions. This mix is most often found in health food stores. Serve with butter and maple syrup.

Italian Tomato-Basil Strata

This meatless breakfast dish is a color hit. The red, creamy white, and bright green is just a knockout. Vegetarians can partake as well. Also check out the other breakfast dishes in the New Years Day Brunch menus.

4 plum tomatoes, seeded & diced
½ Cup sun dried tomatoes
2 to 3 Tablespoons fresh basil
6 eggs
2 Cups milk
10 slices of bread
1 teaspoon salt
¼ teaspoon black pepper
2 Cups Mozzarella cheese, shredded

Dice the sun dried tomatoes. If they are the really dry ones, reconstitute in water before adding to the dish. I have never used the ones packed in oil for this recipe. Chop the basil or defrost 2 basil cubes. Whip the eggs and milk. Dice the bread and place in a 9x13 pan that has been sprayed with vegetable spray. Sprinkle cheese over the bread. Whip the eggs, milk, salt and pepper. Add tomatoes and basil. Pour over the bread and cheese. Cover and chill over night. Bake at 350 degrees for 35 to 40 minutes.

Mexican Breakfasts

Living a couple of years in Texas, we learned to appreciate a good Mexican breakfast. Salsa, eggs, Migas, and fresh flour tortillas will warm the soul and fill the stomach for a big day. I make the Chorizo sausage when I buy a pork shoulder and keep it in one-third pound packages in the freezer. I bone the shoulder for a roast and reserve about a pound for this fragrant sausage, or make three meals ahead. One will be the roast stuffed with garlic and fresh rosemary, the second is cubes of pork for grilled pork on a skewer, and the third (of course) some sausage.

Back to the Mexican breakfast: buy or make flour tortillas. Have eggs, chilled boiled potatoes and salsa on hand. With a fruit bowl these recipes make one great brunch. If you are going all the way, Margaritas and Bloody Marys are a must. Of course fresh juice and coffee will be good too.

Chorizo a la Mexicana

1 pound lean pork
1 clove garlic
1 teaspoon salt
2 Tablespoons chili powder
1 teaspoon dried oregano
2 Tablespoons cider vinegar

Grind pork to coarse or use plain ground pork with no seasonings. Add all other ingredients and mix by hand (wear a plastic glove as the ingredients will stain your nails and skin). Cover and let stand in the refrigerator for several hours.

Use 1/3 pound of sausage, browned with 4 eggs whipped and then scrambled together. Stuff into warm flour tortillas and serve immediately. Makes 8 soft breakfast tacos.

Migas

After a couple of visits to "Trudy's Café Breakfast Anytime" in Austin, the components of this Tex-Mex treat came to light. With fried potatoes on the side and a flour tortilla or two, this could be a great meatless supper dish too.

4 corn tortillas
½ large bell pepper
1 medium onion
1 medium tomato
4 eggs
½ Cup shredded Colby/Jack cheese
Oil

Tear corn tortillas into pieces about one inch by one inch. Cut bell pepper and onion into similar size pieces. Dice tomato into ½ inch dice. Set aside vegetables and tortillas until ready to prepare. Heat 2 Tablespoons oil in large fry pan. Fry corn tortillas until crisp but not brown. Sauté onions and peppers until crisp-tender. Stir in tomatoes and heat through. Whip 4 eggs and scramble with tortilla pieces and vegetable. When nearly firm, sprinkle cheese on top of eggs. Turn heat off and let heat from pan melt the cheese. Serve immediately with salsa and flour tortillas.

Egg and Potato Soft Tacos

3 or 4 medium potatoes
4 eggs
8 flour tortillas
Oil, salt and pepper
Salsa

Boil potatoes to tender, drain and chill. Remove skins. Slice. Fry in oil until golden brown. Season the potatoes with salt and pepper. Whip 4 eggs. Prepare like scrambled eggs over the potatoes. Serve immediately in flour tortillas with salsa.

Western Omelet

What's a he-man fighter pilot most likely to eat before flying a mission? A hearty breakfast at home was usually too early for Tony. Since the first flights took off at sunrise, that meant he had to be in the squadron briefing two hours before takeoff, and because we lived off base, that meant leaving the driveway sometimes at 3:30. Besides that, Tony really didn't like breakfast foods, so by the time the flight briefing was complete he was ready for something. His favorite? Two frozen burritos and a coke! His next favorite eventually became this recipe.

3 eggs
1 Tablespoon butter
1 teaspoon vegetable oil
¼ bell pepper thinly sliced
1 Tablespoon diced onion
2 or 3 sliced mushrooms
¼ Cup minced ham
¼ shredded sharp cheddar cheese

Beat eggs to fluffy and set aside. Heat an omelet pan and add butter and oil. Cook until butter stops foaming. Sauté the vegetables in the pan. Add the ham and heat through. Remove from pan and set aside. Return the pan to the heat. Fluff up the eggs and slide into the pan. When the omelet is set return the veggies and ham to the top of the omelet. Sprinkle the cheese over the top. Fold in half and slip from the pan. Share this with someone special with toast, juice and coffee. A little picante sauce over the top is the perfect touch.

III. Main Dishes

The main dish of the career was now upon us. Having demonstrated to all that Tony could live the life of a Tactical Air Command pilot and handle an airplane reasonably well, he earned an assignment into the A-10. The training pipeline for this aircraft was about six months long, and was conducted at Davis-Monthan AFB near Tucson, Arizona. The airplane was fairly easy to fly, but since it was single seat, the very first flight was solo. The instructor flies his own aircraft (another A-10) just a few feet behind the student aircraft in what is called "chasing tailpipes", a well-known task in the single-seat fighter community.

Following training we arrived in Alexandria, Louisiana, having been assigned to the 23ʳᵈ Tactical Fighter Wing, and the 74ᵗʰ Tactical Fighter Squadron (the Flying Tigers). The squadron was tight-knit and we had wonderful opportunities to socialize and enjoy true Cajun cooking. Some of our favorite get-togethers were out behind our house doing a crab boil with say 50-100 pounds of crawfish (heads-on of course). Louisiana was both a very friendly place and not so friendly at times, as this would be the first place that Tony would be shot at in the airplane. Seems some folks who lived in the area didn't cotton too much to them noisy airplanes flying over their houses, and one day Tony came back from a flight with a couple gunshot holes in the tail.

Tony also had the opportunity to fly in a Maple Flag exercise, held annually at Canadian Forces Base Cold Lake, Canada. While the flying was great, they also enjoyed their hosts and the local area a lot, taking the opportunity to try ice fishing. What a great time he had, standing on top of a frozen lake, with a line tied to a bat and a spoon to the other end. They found a hole drilled thru the ice, dipped the rig into the water, and watched the fish come up to the spoon and bite it. Once hooked, they yanked the fish out of the water then swacked it over the head with the bat. They caught seventeen Northern Pike in a couple hours, took them back to clean, and then packed and froze them for the return trip to Louisiana. On the fourth of July, we all got together again and had a cookout at our house for all the anglers on that trip. While Pike is normally a little bony, between the freezing and the deep frying, the tiny bones just disappeared when we used the fried fish recipe later in this chapter. The fish was so good, some of the guys didn't care about the bones. Mikey Cook said it best, "If you just chew a little longer, you can hardly tell there's any bones at all!"

Eye of Round
(Beef with Bordelaise Sauce)
Serves 15-16

Make the roast only and slice very thinly (an electric meat slicer works great) for the very best French Dip Sandwiches ever. Serve thinly sliced with the Bordelaise Sauce, steamed rice and a green vegetable and you'll have a dinner party worthy dish. Just remember that the oven door stays closed for one hour after you have turned off the heat. No peeking!

5-6 pounds eye of round roasts
Tony's Creole seasoning or any other spicy seasoned salt
Worcestershire sauce   (see Chapter 6)

Shake Worcestershire sauce liberally over meat and then massage in. Sprinkle Creole seasoning over meat (use a little for mild-spicy flavor, use a lot for bolder tastes). Preheat oven to 500 degrees, place roast on rack in oven and bake at 7 minutes a pound for the largest roast. Then turn off oven; leave the door closed at least 1 hour. Serve warm with Bordelaise Sauce. Serve cold with mustards, horseradish, and small rolls. The roast will be medium rare. For medium to well done add 2 minutes per pound to the cooking time.

Bordelaise Sauce

2 Cups red wine
2 Cups beef broth
¾ pounds fresh mushrooms, sliced
½ Cup yellow onion, minced
3-4 cloves of garlic, chopped
2 Tablespoons olive oil
4 Tablespoons parsley
Black pepper
2 Tablespoons cornstarch mixed with 4 Tablespoons water

Place wine and beef broth together in sauce pan and reduce the liquid to half. Sauté the sliced mushrooms, crushed garlic, and yellow onion in olive oil until tender. Stir into the reduced wine and beef broth. Add parsley and pepper. If you used canned broth don't add salt. If you made your own broth, salt to taste. Let this sit until nearly serving time. Bring to boil and thicken with cornstarch mixture.

Rump Roast

Coat the meat with seasoned flour and brown in some oil. Don't burn, but brown all sides, then pour off oil. Put rack in bottom of same pan, add ½ inch water, sprinkle minced dried onions over top of roast, pinch of salt, and pepper, then cover and cook at 350 degrees for 3 hours. Ensure water is always in bottom. Add more water during cooking as necessary.

Serve with cooked carrots, boiled potatoes and gravy made from the drippings.

<u>Corned Beef</u>

When selecting a corned beef at the meat counter, I prefer the ones that are seasoned with some herbs and spices. There's usually some bay leaf, a few mustard seeds, a little red pepper and so forth swimming around with the meat juices. Often the spices are in a separate cellophane bag.

1 corned beef
Water
1 head of cabbage, cut into wedges
1 pound of carrots, peeled and cut into 2 inch pieces
2 medium onions cored
4 ribs of celery cut into 2 inch pieces
4 large red potatoes, quartered or a bunch of new potatoes
2 large turnips peeled and quartered

Start cooking 2 ½ to 3 hours before you're ready to serve.
Slip the corned beef, juice and seasonings into a large kettle cover with plenty of water and simmer for at least 2 hours. Check for tenderness by piercing with a pot fork. A larger corned beef may take a little longer. Above all, don't let the meat cook at a hard boil. You might as well serve shredded sweat socks.
Now, here's the reason that you used such a big pot. Put all the vegetables into the pot with the cabbage on top. Increase the heat to bring to a slow boil. Then reduce the heat and cook all the vegetables until just tender. Cook them too long and you will have mush.
Lift out the corned beef. Let it rest for 10 minutes or so before slicing across the grain to serve. Arrange the meat and vegetables on a big platter with sides. The vegetables are pretty juicy. Serve with mustard, horseradish and butter on the table for garnishing. If there are any leftovers, they reheat well. And what's better than a corned beef sandwich on rye with mustard for lunch later in the week?

Cornish Pasties

One year we took a walking tour of the Lizard Coast of England (something we highly recommend). We found these meat pies to be quite interesting, but sometimes a challenge to prepare well without them coming out soupy. Ensure the edges of the crust are sealed really well to keep the juices in. Using a double interlocking fold is best.

1 recipe Short Crust Pastry (next page)
1 pound round steak or lean pork, diced
1 Cup potatoes, peeled and diced
¾ Cup finely chopped onion
1 teaspoon thyme
2 Tablespoons scotch
½ teaspoon dry mustard
1 teaspoon salt
½ teaspoon pepper
¼ Cup finely chopped parsley
Butter
1 egg, lightly beaten

Preheat oven to 350 degrees. Roll out pastry thinly and cut into 5 inch rounds. Mix together steak potatoes, onion, thyme, scotch, mustard, salt, pepper and parsley. Place 3 Tablespoons mixture in center of each round. Dot with butter.

Moisten edges of pastry and fold dough over filling to make pillow shapes; seal edges with fork. Cut 2 small slits in top and brush with beaten egg. Place on baking sheet and bake 40-50 minutes or until pasties are golden brown. Serve warm with a fresh salad, vegetables, and a tankard of ale or your favorite beer. Yield 8.

Short Crust Pastry

3 Cups all purpose flour
1 ½ teaspoons salt
1 Cup butter (2 sticks)
8-9 Tablespoons ice water

Mix together flour and salt, cut in butter and mix thoroughly. Sprinkle in ice water by tablespoonfuls and blend to form firm dough. Chill before rolling.

Crustless Crab Quiche

1 small onion, diced
1 red pepper, diced
2 Cups mushrooms, sliced
2 eggs
1 Cup low fat cottage cheese
¼ Cup yogurt
½ Cup low fat sour cream
Salt
Pepper
¼ teaspoon cayenne pepper
¾ Cup sharp cheddar cheese, grated
¼ Cup Romano cheese, grated
1 Cup crab (canned, frozen or fresh)

Sauté onion and red pepper, set aside. Sauté sliced mushrooms. Mix eggs, cottage cheese, yogurt, flour, sour cream, dash of salt and pepper, and cayenne pepper. Blend until stiff. Fold in crab, onions peppers and cheeses. Bake 40 minutes in a 350 degree oven.

Whole Baked Fish

The dressing:

½ onion, minced
½ stalk celery, minced
1 carrot, matchstick Julienne (about ¾ Cup)
1 Cup vegetable or chicken stock
3 Cups fresh bread cubes from day old bread
½ teaspoon thyme
1 small clove garlic
1 teaspoon parsley
Salt & pepper

Sauté vegetables adding the garlic last so it doesn't burn. Place the bread cubes, the herbs and the sautéed vegetables in a mixing bowl. Moisten with stock, season with salt & pepper. If you've used canned stock, don't over-salt. Place in bottom of 9x13 inch pan and place fish fillets over, or set aside to stuff the whole fish.

The fish:
Season the outside of the fish by rubbing with a little oil and sprinkle with Tony's seasoning (Chapter 6). For fillets on top of the dressing, bake at 350 for 15-20 minutes until the fish is firm. If stuffing a whole fish, score the thickest part of the fish with a sharp knife, bake at 10 minutes per pound for each inch of thickness at the thickest part of the fish. Add 10 minutes for the dish itself. Cover the tail of the fish with aluminum foil to keep it from burning. Pour either stock or ½ cup white wine around the fish in the pan to minimize sticking, and assists steaming.

Fish Creole

This is a great one-pan dish for just about any kind of thick-fleshed fish you can catch. We use it a lot with shark. The sauce can be made up ahead of time and when you're ready to eat, heat it up and pop the fish in for a few minutes until it firms up. Vary the seasonings a bit to cool it down, or spice it up. Change the fish to shrimp and you have Shrimp Creole.

2 ribs celery
½ - ¾ Cup bell pepper
½ large onion
Garlic
2 bay leaves
1 teaspoon dried thyme
1 teaspoon dried basil
1 Tablespoon parsley
1 16oz can diced tomatoes
½ teaspoon Creole seasoning

Chop the celery, bell pepper and onion. Sauté celery, onion and bell pepper until limp. Add dried herbs, then add garlic last, and sauté for a minute more. Add 1 can diced tomatoes (and a can of tomato sauce for a thicker sauce), and simmer 20 min. Add fish and cook for a few minutes until fish is cooked/firm. Check it at 3 minutes. Five minutes might be too long.
Serve with basmati rice or any long grain rice.

Hot Tuna Sandwiches

8-ounce can of Chunk Light Tuna in water
1 Rib Celery, finely diced
½ Cup sliced, stuffed olives
4-ounces Velveeta, cut into ½ cubes
2 Tablespoons Miracle Whip
4 hoagie rolls

Preheat oven to 350 degrees. Drain the tuna and toss with celery, olives, and Velveeta . Moisten with Miracle Whip. Fill the rolls with the tuna mixture. Wrap in aluminum foil. Place on cookie sheet and heat in oven for 15 minutes or until the cheese melts.

Fried Fish with Tartar Sauce

Fresh water fish are usually handled differently than salt-water fish. This recipe is great for bass, white perch, pike, catfish or crappy. If you are allergic to mustard, soak the fish in buttermilk and proceed.

1 pound fish fillets
¼ Cup salad mustard
1 can beer
½ Cup all purpose flour
½ Cup yellow corn meal
1 teaspoon Creole seasoning
1 Cup Miracle Whip
¼ Cup sweet pickle relish
Juice of ½ a lemon
Oil for frying

Rinse the fillets. Dry on paper towels. Set aside. Mix mustard and ¼ can of beer in a container large enough to hold all the fish. Add the fish. Add more beer to make sure the fish are all coated with mustard and beer. In a flat bowl mix flour, cornmeal and seasoning. Set aside. Combine Miracle Whip, relish and lemon juice in a small bowl. Refrigerate until time to use.

Heat oil to 350 degrees. Shake the excess mustard mixture from the fish. Dredge fish pieces one at a time in the coating mixture. Fry to a light brown in deep fat or shallow pan with ½ inch of oil. Drain pieces and continue frying until are pieces are cooked.

Serve with tartar sauce on the side and a wedge of lemon.

Chioppino, Fish Stew

Fish Stew is the perfect meal for a crowd. The only problem is that the majority of the cooking is done just before the dish is eaten. Sauté the veggies and make the sauce ahead of time. Then the seafood will only take a few minutes to cook. When serving, make sure that vessels for discarded shells are available to all diners. Other important tools are the seafood crackers -- inexpensive nutcrackers work well. I serve linguini and crusty bread on the side with this dish.

1 large onion, ¼ inch dice
3-4 ribs of celery, crosscut ½ inch
1 large bell pepper, ¼ inch dice
2 Cups carrots, ¼ inch dice
2 to 3 Tablespoons olive oil
4-6 cloves of garlic, minced
2 bay leaves
4 basil cubes (Chapter 6)
1 teaspoon salt
½ teaspoon black pepper
3 Cups canned tomato sauce
2 1-pound canned diced tomatoes
1 quart chicken stock
1 Cup dry white wine
1 pound shrimp, shells on
2 pounds mussels or small clams
1 pound firm white fleshed fish (shark), 1 inch dice
2 to 3 pounds crab legs (optional)
½ Cup fresh chopped parsley

Get out your big kettle. Scrub all the shells of the seafood, rinse and set aside in the refrigerator. Sauté the onion, celery, bell pepper, and carrots in the olive oil until the onion is translucent. Add the garlic and bay leaves and continue the sauté for a couple more minutes. Do not burn the garlic. Add the basil cubes, tomato sauce, diced tomatoes and chicken stock and simmer for 10 to 15 minutes. Stir in the white wine and cook for 5 more minutes. This is the time to adjust the seasoning keeping in mind that the fish will add a bit of salt to the pot. 5 minutes prior to serving have the stew at the near boil. Add the shrimp, mussels, crab and fish. Cook until the mussels open and the other seafood is opaque.

Goulash

Early marriage recipes like this one occasionally stay with us. This definitely fits in the comfort food range. It makes a great middle of the week meal. Double it and there are leftovers for another night.

½ pound ground beef
½ onion, chopped
Bell pepper, diced
1 15-ounce can diced tomatoes
1 small can V-8 juice (6 ounces)
Salt & pepper to taste
2 Cups uncooked pasta

Brown ground beef and chopped onion. Sauté with bell pepper. Add tomatoes and V-8. Salt and Pepper. Simmer about 30 minutes minimum.

Boil pasta such as elbow macaroni or shells in lots of water until al dente. Drain. Add pasta to the ground beef mixture. Adjust the seasonings. Serve with green salad and buttered bread. Tony likes a little Italian cheese on his serving.

Gray Stuff

True comfort food! Our son Nick will only eat this with canned peas. I guess it has something to do with the taste. To dress up the dish you can make homemade noodles. Garnish with freshly chopped parsley.

1½ pounds ground beef
¼ Cup minced dried onions
1 large can mushrooms with juice
Salt, pepper, parsley
2 teaspoons Worcestershire
1 Can mushroom soup
8 ounces sour cream
8 ounces egg noodles

Brown the beef; add mushrooms, onions, salt and pepper to taste, sprinkle Worcestershire seasoning and add can of mushroom soup and parsley. Stir together and heat throughout. Simmer 10 minutes or so to have the flavors blend. Add cooked noodles and sour cream, serve hot.

Herbed Baked Salmon

1 ½ pounds salmon, cut in thick slabs
3 ounces Parmesan, grated
6 Tablespoons minced green onions
3 Tablespoons chopped fresh: basil, dill, parsley, chervil, thyme
2 Tablespoons red bell pepper, minced
Juice 1/2 lemon
Salt, fresh ground pepper, cayenne pepper

Preheat oven to 350F. Mix cheese, onions, herbs pepper lemon, salt, pepper, cayenne in small bowl. Spread on the non-skin side of salmon filet almost to edge. Spray shallow baking dish with non-stick spray and warm in oven 20 min. Place salmon skin side down on dish and sizzle. Bake 20 min or until flaky.

Horseshoe Sandwich

The Horseshoe was a staple on the luncheon menu of the Royal Room at the Holiday Inn in Urbana, Illinois where we first lived during college. It can be made with turkey, ham, or shrimp. The sandwich was surrounded with hand cut French Fries, which resembled a horseshoe shape.

2 Cup leftover turkey
2 Tablespoons margarine
2 Tablespoons flour
1 to 1 ¼ Cup milk
4 ounces Velveeta
Toasted bread
½ Cup shredded sharp cheddar
Sprinkle of paprika, salt & pepper

Cut or tear up turkey and set aside. Melt margarine and stir in flour. Stir in milk, whisk, & bring to boil. Then cook for 1 additional minute. Break Velveeta into small pieces & stir into milk. Melt cheese. Season with salt & pepper. Add turkey and heat through. Assemble sandwich open faced on the toasted bread with meat and cheese. Sprinkle shredded cheese & paprika over the top. Place under broiler until cheese bubbles. Serve at once. Makes 2.

Korean Ribs (Kalbi)

Two assignments in Korea gave the Giacobe Family an appreciation for some of the Korean fare. Luckily during the second tour, one of the Korean-American wives taught me the rudiments of these dishes. We usually have rice, Chop Chae, Yaki Mandu, and Kimchi with the ribs. Buy the Kimchi in a jar in the Asian market. Throw out what you don't use the day you open it, as it will dominate your refrigerator for sure.

If it's the day after Thanksgiving, it has to be Korean Ribs, Kalbi. These are quite different from western ribs. The meat is crosscut beef chuck rib. I like ¾ of an inch thick. Half inch is acceptable, but quarter inch thick ones are too thin. There will be 3 oval shaped bones on each strip of rib meat. Be sure to have beer with this dinner. Start working on this one three to four days in advance.

Kalbi

1 Cup soy sauce
½ large onion, pureed
10 cloves garlic, minced
3 to 4 Tablespoons sesame oil
½ Cup red wine
2 Tablespoons toasted sesame seeds
3 to 4 Tablespoons sugar
1 bunch green onions, thinly angle sliced
3 pounds cross cut ribs

Mix all ingredients thoroughly with exception of ribs. Trim as much of the fat off the ribs as you can. This will help nutritionally as well as keeping the barbeque from flaring up. Place ribs in plastic or glass container. Pour marinade over the meat, cover and refrigerate. Stir daily for at least 2 days, preferably 3 days. This is important, as the marinade is what is actually going to cook the meat. Placing it on the grill simply heats it up and completes the cooking process. Grill over medium heat until medium to medium rare. Serve while hot.

Chop Chae

4 ounces beef chuck or round
1 package Sweet Potato Starch Noodles
2 small or 1 large zucchini
1 large carrot
4 cloves garlic
1 medium onion
¼ Cup soy sauce

Look for some of these ingredients at the Asian Market or your favorite grocery store in the specialty ingredients section

2-3 Tablespoons toasted sesame seeds
Canola oil for stir frying
½ bunch green onions
2 to 3 Tablespoons sesame oil
8 Shitake mushrooms

This dish requires **excellent** knife skills or a V-slicer. Pound the meat thin. Shred with knife about eighth inch thick strips. Set aside. Angle slice zucchini and stack slices to slice angle into ¼ inch Julienne. Carrots and mushrooms are done in the same fashion only 1/8 inch thick. Make 1/8-inch thick slices of onion. Use a garlic press for garlic or mash and finely mince. Thinly angle slice the green onion. If you have a V-slicer, use it for the onions, zucchini and carrots. Select appropriate blades. Do the vegetables ahead and keep in small plastic bags, or have your guests work like apprentices in the kitchen with you.

The most difficult part of this dish is buying the noodles. In a Korean market ask someone in the noodle aisle to help you find noodles for Chop Chae. Boil the noodles like spaghetti. Drain and rinse. The noodles can be cooked ahead and kept in the refrigerator for a couple of hours. Do not be shocked: the noodles are a clear gray when cooked.

Chop Chae can be eaten either hot or at room temperature. I prefer it hot. While Tony is grilling the ribs and the rice is nearly cooked, it's time to assemble the Chop Chae. Use a very big skillet or wok. Heat a couple of Tablespoons of Canola Oil to very hot. Stir fry the meat and remove. Add a bit more oil and stir fry the vegetable beginning with the carrots, then the onion, garlic and finally the zucchini. Cook the vegetable Asian style leaving a bit of texture but not raw or soft and mushy. Stir in soy sauce and green onion. Return meat to the pan and mix in the noodles. Season with the sesame oil and sesame seeds.

A lot of kids like the spaghetti version of this dish. Do everything above, but reserve some of the vegetable meat mixture before throwing in the cellophane noodles. Set aside in a separate bowl, and mix in with regular spaghetti. The kids will love it as you enjoy the Korean version.

Bulgogi

Bulgogi is probably the national meat dish of Korea. Served with rice and kimchi, but of course everything in Korea is served with rice and kimchi. In Korean restaurants, you're seated on the floor, cross-legged, at a table with a miniature barbeque in the center. They bring hot coals, numerous varieties of kimchis to munch on, and a plate of the Bulgogi. Scissors are used to cut the meat into small portions, and everybody cooks their own. It is sort of like Fondue over the grill.

When our friends Warner & Cindy came to Korea to visit us on their honeymoon, it was the only entrée that Warner would order. Of course, he could never remember the name of it, so he would always ask us, "What's the name of the dinner that I like?", and the three of us would answer in unison "Bulgogi". "That's what I'm going to have then" was his reply. If you're making a big Korean meal with Kalbi, just pour the marinade off the ribs and use it on the Bulgogi.

Start with thinly sliced (across the grain) beef chuck. Use the marinade that is the same for the Kalbi (Korean ribs) for about an hour. Then place on the grill and cook (slowly if you can) until done. Avoid flare-ups, as the meat will burn quite easily. This should only take a few minutes. If it dries up, it's overcooked. Use 2 pounds of lean chuck (like in a shoulder roast) to 2 cups of the marinade to serve 4 to 6 adults.

Italian Sausage

Living a little bit of everywhere meant that we collected recipes and cooking techniques from many places. Finding specific foods or ingredients could be challenging. Flour tortillas are very hard to find in Korea. Italian Sausage was difficult to find in Oklahoma. And a crusty loaf of real French bread was only made at home in lots of places. So when you have a pork roast that is too big or you just want to know exactly what's in your sausage, try this recipe. If you want it hotter add more red pepper flakes. Be sure to add some fat when you are grinding really lean pork. Without the fat the sausage will be dry and tasteless.

2 ¼ pounds coarse ground pork
1 teaspoon fennel seeds
1 bay leaf
2 Tablespoons dried parsley
2 to 3 cloves garlic
1 teaspoon red pepper flakes
1 teaspoon salt
1 Tablespoon water
½ teaspoon black pepper

Mix well with hands and let rest in the refrigerator for 1 hour or more before use. Best to rest overnight. Use within three days or freeze. When using fat back to increase the amount of fat in the sausage, rinse thoroughly, cut into ½ inch strips and reduce salt to one teaspoon.

Meat Loaf

Serve this up for dinner, then slice the cold leftovers for sandwiches. We usually have mashed potatoes and green beans along side for dinner. When our son Drew moved to California, he called the gravy "Secret Sauce." His health conscious West Coast friends would eat plates of this stuff. Of course later he made it with ground turkey when he got off beef. One night my best friend Cindy, made the meat loaf for her son Will, and did not make the sauce. He was mortified. "Mrs. G always made the sauce, Mom."

1 ½ pounds ground beef
2 eggs
½ to ¾ Cup oatmeal or crumbs
2 Tablespoons minced dried onions
2 Tablespoons dry parsley
½ teaspoon salt
¼ teaspoon black pepper
½ of a 12 ounce can milk
Water, if too dry

Shape into loaf. Mixture should be moist when formed. Bake uncovered 45 minutes at 350 degrees. Pour off excess fat. Stir together 1 can cream of mushroom soup mixed with about half a can of evaporated milk. Bake ½ hour more at 350 degrees.

Meatball Recipe

Tony's Aunt Grace was born in Italy. She had her own recipe, and really made the day when she accidentally threw whole cloves of garlic in, instead of mincing it. These "loaded centers" were really a surprise, and tended to linger a loooooooooong time.

Later, when I worked in radio and TV in Alexandria Louisiana, I enjoyed frequent guest appearances on the "Great Day in the Morning" show with TV host Bill Day. We did a lot of

*cooking, and had a lot of fun too. I featured this recipe on one of
the morning shows.*

Basically this has the same ingredients as meatloaf, but add
½- teaspoon dried basil and garlic. Use small ice cream scoop
(melon ball size), and roll individual balls with damp hands. Place
on cookie sheet, then bake at 350 degrees. When firm and lightly
browned, remove from pan with spatula, and serve/store/ add to
other dishes.

Pork Chops with Sage Dressing

½ onion minced
1 stalk celery, diced
2-3 Tablespoons ground sage
1 Tablespoon margarine or butter
1 Tablespoon oil
3 Cups herbed stuffing cubes
2 Cups vegetable or chicken stock
Optional: 1 medium granny apple, diced 1 inch cubes

Melt butter or margarine in pan, add oil, and then sauté
vegetables. Add stuffing cubes, moisten with stock, season with
sage, salt & pepper. The dressing should be a little on the wet side,
because it will dry as it bakes. Let it sit long enough to absorb the
moisture, since they are so dry. Spray a baking dish to prevent
sticking, and fill with dressing. Place ¾ inch thick pork chops on
top of the dressing. Season them with salt, pepper and garlic
powder, drizzle about 1 teaspoon honey on top of each chop. Bake
at 350 degrees for 30-40 minutes uncovered.

Pork Chops & Apples

6 1-inch thick boneless pork chops
Flour
Salt & pepper
2 Tablespoons olive oil
6 small or 3 large apples, sliced, skins on
1/2 Cup brown sugar

Dredge the pork chops through the seasoned flour mixture, and pan fry in about a tablespoon of oil, ensuring all sides are browned. While the chops are cooking, core and slice the apples and set aside. When the chops are nicely browned, add the apple slices and brown sugar, and sauté at medium heat with lid on. Stir every 4 –5 minutes until the apples are tender but not soggy. Drain the juice from the pan or sieve out the apples and serve separately.

Pork Roast with Rosemary

6-8 inch long boneless pork loin
1/3 Cup fresh rosemary
3 cloves chopped garlic
½ - 1 teaspoon salt
fresh ground black pepper

Trim the loin of excess fat. Place the roast fat-side-up in a roasting pan. Score the fat so the flavors can penetrate the meat. In a mortar and pestle, grind the salt, rosemary leaves, and garlic together. Mix in fresh cracked black pepper. Spread on top of pork loin. Roast at 350 degrees until done, or 160 degrees internal (about 20-25 minutes per pound).

Reuben Sandwich

Add a Kosher pickle on the side with a few chips or some potato salad and you will have a sandwich plate to rival any deli. Either cook the corned beef yourself or purchase it. Of course the home cooked will be lower in salt, more tender and leaner. This makes a big lunch for one or a lighter lunch for two.

Thin slices of corned beef
2 Slices of rye bread with caraway seeds
1 can sauerkraut
Slices of Swiss cheese
Thousand Island salad dressing
Butter or margarine

Drain and rinse the sauerkraut and drain again. Spread the rye bread with butter. The outside of sandwich will get the butter like a grilled cheese. Spread the inside of the bread with a generous amount of Thousand Island Dressing. Top with approximately ¼ to 1/3 cup of sauerkraut on each piece of bread. Top with the thin slices of cheese. Grill the bread portions in a medium hot skillet until nicely browned and cheese begins to melt. Heat the corned beef thoroughly by grilling or in the microwave. Stack the meat on the grilled bread, dressing, sauerkraut and cheese. Cover with the other grilled bread portion. Cut into 2 pieces.

<u>Ribs</u>

These are not delicate little baby back ribs. These are the big spare ribs. They should be cooked to that perfect state of almost tender enough to fall off the bone, but not quite that much. Seasoning is important. Sauce is a last minute thing. The very best ribs I have ever eaten came from Champaign, Illinois. The spot was Po Boys. I also liked their potato salad and creamy slaw. A close second was a full slab of baby back ribs from the Homestead Restaurant in Kankakee, Illinois back in the 80's. Every time we visited my family there, we ate at the Homestead and Tony would always order the ribs. So when we were in Korea, we would occasionally get a BBQ sauce-stained napkin in the mail just to remind us what we were missing.

1 slab of spare ribs
Creole seasoning
Kraft Original Barbeque Sauce

With a sharp knife cut between the rib bones and separate into single ribs. Generously sprinkle the ribs with the Creole seasoning. Place the ribs in a roasting pan with rack. Cover and bake at 350 for 1 to 1 ½ hours. Remove to the grill. Dip each rib in the sauce and place on a medium hot grill. Grill until the sauce is set but not burned. Serve with corn on the cob, potato salad and slaw.

Pot Roast

I used to make this at least once a week when the boys were at home. When I was working, I would set the timers on the oven to start the roast at the appropriate time to be ready when I got home. I would start with a frozen roast in the morning. By the time the oven came on, it was thawed and ready to go. Serve with potatoes, cooked carrots or make the Yorkshire pudding instead of potatoes. Cut up leftover roast and place in gravy with chunks of fresh potato, carrots and green beans. Cook until potatoes are tender. Adjust thickness of gravy and you have stew.

1 arm bone or 7-bone roast, boneless or bone-in
¼ Cup dry minced onions
Salt & pepper
1 Cup water
5 to 6 Tablespoons flour
Water

Place the meat in a roasting pan with rack in bottom and a lid that fits the pan snugly. Sprinkle meat with the onions and salt and pepper. Pour water in bottom of pan. Cover with the lid. Roast in a 350 degree oven for 1 ½ to 2 hours. Remove meat to platter. Remove rack scrapping off any brown bits. Scrape onion mixture off top and return to roasting pan. Make a slurry of flour and water for the gravy. Pour into drippings stirring constantly. Add more water as need for correct gravy consistency.

Salmon Patties with Pea Gravy

For many years salmon was a staple in the pantry. This was especially true if you grew up in a Roman Catholic home. The salmon was served on those meatless Fridays. This slightly updated version of a family favorite will serve 2 or 3 people with mashed potatoes.

1 8-ounce canned red salmon
2 Tablespoons onion, finely minced
10 to 12 crushed saltine crackers
1 egg, well beaten
¼ 10-ounce can evaporated milk

Drain the water from the salmon. Give the water to your cat. Mash-up the salmon, and remove the larger pieces of skin and bones. Mix all the ingredients together. Shape patties and chill.
Pan fry in vegetable oil until light brown over medium high heat. Eat with tartar sauce, cheese sauce or my favorite, pea gravy.

Pea Gravy

1 Cup frozen peas
½ Cup water
3 Tablespoons flour and ¼ Cup water
Half a 10-ounce can of evaporated milk
2 Tablespoons Butter

Cook peas to a boil. Mix flour and water into a slurry. Thicken the peas and add milk. Cook at least one minute at the boil. Finish by stirring in the butter.

Beef with Bordelaise pg 42

Pork Chops with Dressing pg 59

Stroganoff pg 52

Stuffed Peppers pg 68

Chicken on a Beer Can pg 75

Chicken Pot Pie pg 86

Chicken Rollups pg 80

Chicken with Grapes pg 77

Fresh Salmon Cakes

Makes approximately 16 (4 ounce) cakes

3 pounds skinless salmon fillets, diced into ¼ inch cubes
2 Cups crumbled Ritz crackers
½ Cup heavy cream
½ red onion, diced
2 cloves garlic, minced
3 Tablespoons chopped fresh dill (or parsley or cilantro)
3 Tablespoons Dijon mustard
3 eggs
1 teaspoon kosher salt
1 Cup flour
½ to ¾ Cup olive oil
2 lemons, each cut into 6 wedges, for garnish

Preheat the oven to 350 degrees. Place everything except the flour, oil and lemons in a large mixing bowl and fold together with a spoon or spatula. Gently form the mixture into ¼ pound "burgers." The mixture will be very loose, and that's the way it should be; you just have to handle it carefully on a dish and flour both sides of the patties.

Next, put about 2 Tablespoons olive oil in a large cast-iron skillet over medium heat. The oil is hot enough when you add a smidgen of flour and it sizzles on contact. Now add a few salmon cakes to the skillet, cooking them until they're golden brown, about 2 to 3 minutes per side. Continue adding oil as needed and cooking the cakes in batches, setting them aside on a sheet pan as they're done.

When you have completed frying the cakes, place the sheet pan in the preheated oven for 5 to 7 minutes until they are warm all the way through. Garnish with the lemon wedges. These can be served on a bun, on a bed of lettuce, or simply on a plate with your favorite side dish.

Shrimp Etouffe

Laura, my Navy wife friend, would prepare a cauldron of Etouffe for Mardi Gras at the U.N. Club in Korea. It was one of those times when we could forget for a little while where we were. One step outside in the freezing cold of a February in Seoul would break the spell. But the flavor of the Etouffe would linger on and on. Yum!

½ pound butter
¼ Cup flour
1 Cup green onion, chopped
2 garlic cloves, minced
1 Cup yellow onion, chopped
½ Cup green pepper, chopped
½ Cup celery, chopped
3 Cups liquid*
1 bay leaf
¼ teaspoon thyme
1 teaspoon basil
8 ounces tomato sauce
½ teaspoon pepper
2 teaspoons salt
2 Tablespoons Worcestershire sauce
2 pounds shrimp
1 teaspoon lemon juice
1 teaspoon grated lemon rind
¼ Cup parsley

* (Liquid is 1 Cup wine plus 2 Cups fish bouillon or 1 Cup wine plus 1 Cup fish bouillon plus 1 Cup water)

Make a walnut colored roux with ¼ pound butter and flour. Add onions, garlic, green pepper, celery, bay leaf, thyme, basil and remaining butter. Sauté uncovered, for 30 minutes over medium heat. Add tomato sauce, pepper, salt, Worcestershire sauce and liquid. Bring to boil, reduce heat and simmer slowly, uncovered for 1 hour, stirring occasionally. Add shrimp and cook 10 minutes. Remove from heat. Add lemon juice, rind and parsley. Place in refrigerator. Remove 1 hour before serving, reheat without boiling. Serve over rice.

Sloppy Joes

No matter what kind of bun you use, no matter how carefully you eat these, a Sloppy Joe will drip down the front of your shirt. It's just a fact of life. If the sandwich didn't drip, it just would not be a Sloppy Joe.

1 ½ pounds of ground beef
1 medium onion, diced
1 bell pepper diced
¼ Cup brown sugar
1 16-ounce can tomato sauce
1 16-ounce can diced tomatoes, drained and reserved
1 Tablespoon chili powder
1 teaspoon Salt
Pepper to taste

Brown the ground beef. Drain excess fat. Add the onion and pepper. Sauté until tender. Add the rest of the ingredients and simmer covered for 30 to 45 minutes. If the mixture becomes too thick use the reserve juice from the tomatoes to thin. Serve on your favorite rolls or buns. Serves at least 4 boys.

Stuffed Peppers

When Tony and I were first married I made stuffed peppers. He ate the stuffing out of 3 or 4 and left the peppers for me. It was years until I made them again. We have grown many different colored bell peppers in our home garden and find the squatty flat-bottomed ones work best. The longer more slender ones need to be split length wise and then stuffed. No matter which color pepper you use or how many different colors you use at one time, they all cook about the same. Choose peppers that are all about the same size and shape.

6 large bell peppers
1 pound ground beef
1 egg
½ Cup minced fresh onion
Salt and pepper
½ Cup milk
2 Cups leftover rice or rice pilaf
2 Tablespoons minced parsley
Tomato Sauce

Clean and wash the peppers. Cut the tops off, scoop out the seeds and membranes, set aside. Mix together like making a meatloaf: the ground beef, egg, onion, salt, pepper, and milk. Add the rice and parsley. Stuff the ground beef mixture into the bottom of the peppers. Spoon some tomato sauce (store bought is fine) over the mixture. Put the lids on top. Place in oven proof baking dish. Pour hot water around bases of peppers about 1 inch high. Bake at 350 degree until meat thermometer registers 160 degrees. Serve one large or 2 small peppers per person.

Beef Tongue

Growing-up in a farm family with a mother of Canadian-French heritage and father of German heritage meant that we ate everything except the oink, moo, and cluck. Then of course there were all the other things that didn't seem to make noises that we ate as well. When we moved to town, I found most of the people we met were pretty much the white bread and bland folks. Luckily, I met Tony. He was from a family who ate even a larger variety of foods than we did. The foods were the same only seasoned and handled a little differently.

Don't let the title to this dish turn you off. Tongue is really, really tender, and has a wonderful flavor when augmented by the olive-raisin sauce. This recipe comes from both of our families. Tongue was served with brown gravy in my family, and the tomato-raisin-olive sauce is rather Italian.

1 beef tongue	4 to 6 Cups tomato sauce
1 large onion	1 medium onion sliced
2 stalks celery	1 bell pepper sliced
1 bay leaf	½ Cup raisins
6 peppercorns	½ Cup stuffed Spanish olives

Parboil the tongue, i.e., cook in water slowly for a couple of hours to make it tender. This makes it possible to remove the heavy and inedible skin from the top of the tongue. Do this by placing the tongue in a large stockpot with the large onion, celery, bay leaf and peppercorns. Bring to a boil and reduce to a simmer for at least 2 hours. Pierce with a fork to check tenderness. Remove tongue from broth and discard broth. Cool.

Peel the white rubbery skin from tongue. Discard the skin. In a heavy Dutch Oven place the Tomato Sauce, sliced onion, sliced bell pepper, and the raisins. Add the tongue and olives, then simmer until the onions and peppers are soft.

Remove the tongue from the sauce. Slice in quarter inch slices. Serve with the sauce on the side and your favorite pasta.

Roasted Whole Pig

When I first found a recipe for roasting a pig, we lived in Louisiana. The Cajuns roast the pig hanging from a metal tripod and it is turned from head-up to head-down for the last couple hours of cooking. Now, their recipe had style! It said that you start with 3 cases of beer, a case of whiskey, 3 men and begin cooking at midnight. When you run out of beer and whiskey the pig should be done.

This recipe came to me from my OWC friend Joan in Yorktown, Virginia. She's one good cook and the wife of a retired Air Force officer too. It's the kind of meal that you make only a couple of times in your life, but it sure is a kick. Invite 50 to 70 of your closest friends. Have them bring a dish to share. It's a good party. (We use a headless pig in deference to the squeamish.)

1 dressed pig without head, 100-120 pounds
4 well built men
1 large grill
Oven thermometer
Instant read meat thermometer
Mop Sauce
Plain chicken wire, not galvanized or plastic cooked
Large chunks of hickory wood for smoking the meat, soaked

When the pig is ordered ask the butcher to snap the ribs from the spine so that the pig is flat. You want the skin on the pig. Prep the pig by washing with clear water. Place the carcass in the chicken wire and wrap. This will help keep the pig flat and easier to move and turn.

The grill used should be the type you pull behind a pick-up. The charcoal fire should be kept low enough to keep the cooking temperature around 265-275 degrees. Use two fires, one at each end of the grill and have the pig in the middle. This will cook the meat with indirect heat. Place the oven thermometer in the middle of the grill toward the back.

It's time to put the pig on the grill. This is where you need those guys. Put the pig spread-eagle with the skin side up. Now is the time of just making sure that the dripping fat doesn't catch fire. That's all you do for 4 hours. The meat will pull away from the skin. Tap the crusty skin and it will sound hollow.

The pig will cook for about 4 hours before it is turned. Keep the heat constant by adding more charcoal on a regular schedule. After an hour or so of cooking add the hickory to the edge of the fire on each side.

Get the guys back to turn the pig over. After the pig is turned, get out your mop sauce and mop the whole bone side of the pig. After one hour more of cooking check the internal temperature of the hams, the thickest part. I really like an instant read thermometer for this job.

Open the grill and cut-out the ribs and set aside. These are far too good to share with anyone other than your favorite friends or immediate family members as they are the best part of the pig. Take a boning knife and run into the hams and shoulders avoiding breaking the skin. Again mop the pig well. This will use 2 quarts of mop sauce. The rest of the mop sauce will be served with the sliced meat. Keep the fire going "on low" just to keep the meat warm.

When the coleslaw, potato salad and all the fixings are out on the big table, run a knife through the skin and all the fat will drain off. Use a pan filled with cat litter under the grill to catch the fat. Dispose of it so that errant cats and dogs don't get into it.

Get-out the cutting boards, knives and serving pans. And slice up the meat. This is my favorite part of the job.

The most important part of this whole process is having a good time. This recipe goes well with a blue grass band for entertainment. Be sure to invite all the neighbors so they aren't jealous.

Mop Sauce

2 quarts beef stock	1 Tablespoon cayenne pepper
1 Tablespoon garlic powder	1 Tablespoon Tabasco
1 Tablespoon dry mustard	1 Cup vegetable oil
1 Tablespoon chili powder	2 Cups Worcestershire sauce
6 bay leaves	(That's right 2 Cups)
1 Tablespoon paprika	2 Cups cider vinegar

Veal or Steak Oscar

This is an expensive dish to make using either veal or steak. Of course you could save a few dollars raising the calf yourself and teaching the children the fine art of slaughtering and drawing a carcass. (Actually, the class I took in meat science at Kansas State University was one of my favorites.) The first time I ate a version of this dish was at a restaurant in Alexandria, Louisiana. It was an old house that had been converted to a dining establishment. Like much of the South, Alexandria was prone to occasional problems with roaches. This old house was no exception. My friend and I were rather stupid. We simply swatted the nasty creatures off the table and continued eating. If we had only screamed, Karen and I could have had a free dinner.

6 Center-cut veal chops, 1½ to 1¾ inches thick
12 ounces lump crabmeat
2 teaspoons finely minced garlic
2 Tablespoons minced fresh thyme leaves
2 Tablespoons minced fresh parsley
12 ounces fresh asparagus
1 Tablespoon olive oil
Red, white and black pepper
Paprika, parsley sprigs, thyme sprigs

Select chops, trim excess fat, season and prepare for grill. Pick through and season the crab meat with garlic, thyme, parsley, salt and white pepper and a few grains of red pepper. Set aside or refrigerate. Just prior to plating heat quickly in microwave. The crab is already cooked. Wash and trim asparagus spears. Snap spears at end of stem to remove heavy or woody portions. Trim to uniform length. Steam with ½ tablespoon of olive oil added to steaming water. Drain. Keep warm until plating.

Grill the chops and sear on a hot fire. Plate on warmed dinner plates. Top with warmed crabmeat mixture, asparagus spears, and ladle Hollandaise Sauce (Chapter 6) over each portion. Garnish with paprika, parsley sprigs and thyme sprigs. Serve at once.

IV. Chicken Main Dishes

Once we were assigned to New Jersey. When Tony's soon-to-be boss called him to see if he wanted the job, he told him that the best the Air Force could offer at that point was a liaison job with the Civil Air Patrol. Again, not knowing anything about the job, the area, or the mission, Tony said he'd do it. And again, luck was on our side as it turned out to be another flying job, working with some really wonderful people throughout a nine state area all throughout New England. There's an old saying among old fighter pilots: "I'd rather be lucky than good any day." You can be the very best at what you do, but if you're unlucky, the game's over.

Any new assignment takes some learning, and as we got more acquainted with how the Civil Air Patrol worked Tony got really interested in its history. At one point Tony was also doing some genealogical work that his mother had put away long before she died, and while going through some of her U.S. Army things from the mid 1940's, found a small gold set of wings with the three bladed propeller so prominent in today's Civil Air Patrol emblem. Digging deeper and working with the Northeast Region's historian, he found that in 1944 his mom had actually been qualified as a coastal observer in what were then the beginnings of the Civil Air Patrol, while she was waiting in Connecticut to join the Army.

The time we spent in New Jersey gave us some very special opportunities. Tony got his little airplane qualifications updated, and we even joined the aero club. By doing so, we could visit our son and daughter-in-law, Nick and Lisa, in central Pennsylvania,

turning a rather long drive into a ninety minute flight. We also took several trips up the Hudson River, flying just over the Tappanzee Bridge, circling the Statue of Liberty, and looking up at the twin towers of the World Trade Center. Cruising further north we would pass the Palisades, then over the George Washington Bridge, past Sing Sing, and on up to The Academy at West Point, and read the rooftops. Upon returning we would bed down the airplane, then head over to Mastori's restaurant, whose huge portions and outstanding food would always impress our guests. Nobody left Mastori's hungry. It was simply an outstanding afternoon trip, and one that we often shared with visitors.

We also met some very special people in the Civil Air Patrol, their cadet programs, in Aerospace Education, and in their operational search and rescue wings, some who are already no longer with us. Visiting these people who volunteered their time, energy and lives also opened up some lasting friendships as well as some terrific meals. New England lobster on a snowy weekend in New Hampshire is unforgettable. And Al's home cooked breakfast with smothered crepes and cheesecake (almost as good as ours) was an absolute treat.

Of course, this chapter, which is devoted entirely to chicken, has absolutely nothing to do with New Jersey, the Civil Air Patrol, or the fact that Tony was wearing "birds" on his shoulders. It just worked out that way. We have eaten so much chicken that someone would frequently comment, "Well what kind of chicken are we having tonight?" Chicken is a wonderful thing and when cooking isn't rushed, and you don't get it real hot real fast, so it usually turns out very tender, and accepts a wide variety of seasoning. Being inexpensive also means we ate a lot of it, and with the skin and the larger sections of fat removed, it is very healthy. It's a lot of fun to just pick up in your hands and dive into. Just remember to exercise a little care when preparing it, so as not to let it spoil or contaminate anything else in the kitchen. Try many of these recipes outdoors on the grill to keep your kitchen cool.

74

Oven Baked Chicken

Whole chicken cut up into parts, skin on
Salt & pepper
Honey
Powdered garlic

This is a super simple recipe for cooking chicken. Cut up the chicken or use pre-cut parts, skin on. Spray non-stick spray in the bottom of an oven baking dish. Arrange the chicken parts to fit. Season with your favorites, salt & pepper, garlic powder, and then drizzle honey over the parts. Bake in a 325 degree oven for 35 minutes, until golden brown but not burnt. Serve with buttered noodles, green vegetable, and instant gravy.

Chicken on a Beer Can

This is a modification of the Herbed Roasted Chicken recipe (elsewhere in this chapter), and it comes out really moist and tasty. This recipe does very well on a grill.

Prepare the chicken as before, but open a regular size can of beer, place it in a pan or on a rack, and sit the chicken on top of it. Season as desired, but I prefer lots of thyme and some of Tony's seasoning in Chapter 6.

A little water in the pan will help. Bake in a 325 degree oven for 1 ½ - 2 hours, depending on the size of the bird. The beer will evaporate, a very little, and will keep the chicken moist. The chicken will cook a little slower than without the beer can, so adjust accordingly.

Chicken or Shrimp Pasta Alfredo

This is a quick supper from the pantry using a little leftover chicken. You can vary this with choice of vegetable or replace the chicken with a dozen frozen shrimp.

2 Cups leftover roasted chicken or a couple dozen frozen shrimp
1 Tablespoon olive oil
2 Tablespoons butter
4 ounces fresh mushrooms
1 jar creamy Alfredo Sauce
2-3 green onions thinly sliced
Spears of frozen broccoli
12 ounces Florentine Fettuccini
2 ounces white wine
Shredded Italian cheese

Cook pasta according to package directions. Heat large sauté pan with oil and then add butter. Slice and sauté the mushrooms. Add the white portion of the green onions to the mushrooms when they are browned on one side. Continue to sauté until mushroom are browned on both sides and onions are transparent, not browned. Add chicken or shrimp, heating thoroughly before adding the jar of sauce. Place broccoli spears on sides of pan. Pour sauce in the center of the pan. Heat through and simmer. This is where you use the wine. Rinse out the jar with the wine and pour into the pan. Cook until broccoli is crisp-tender and the sauce is hot all through. Drain the pasta. Put on a large platter. Arrange Broccoli along the sides of the pasta. Pour the mushroom and chicken sauce over the noodles. Garnish the top with the thinly sliced green onion tops. Serve at once with cheese as a seasoning.

Chicken with Grapes

Our oldest son calls and asks us, "What kind of chicken did you have for dinner tonight?" Yes, we eat chicken about 3 or 4 times a week. Here's something on the lighter side with a fresh taste that is definitely surprising to guests. Served with noodles and a crisp green salad it makes a handful of grapes and a few chicken breasts rather impressive.

4 chicken breasts
1 Cup dry white wine
¼ Cup cornstarch
¼ Cup flour
Salt and white pepper
1 Cup white grapes
Oil for browning
1 to 1 ½ teaspoons lemon thyme
2 Tablespoons butter

Pound the chicken breast to an even thinness. Mix flour and cornstarch together with salt and pepper in a shallow bowl or plate. Dredge chicken in the mixture. In a large sauté pan with a small amount of oil, brown the chicken to a light golden color. Remove breasts from pan. Add the grapes and lemon thyme. Cook grapes until they begin to blister, but don't pop their skins. Stir in the white wine. Return the chicken to the pan. Reduce the heat and simmer for 5 to 10 minutes, until the chicken is tender. The sauce should thicken on it's own. Remove chicken to serving platter. Whisk in the cold butter and the sauce should be consistency of thin gravy. Spoon the sauce with the grapes over the chicken and serve.

Chicken Breasts in Mushroom Sauce

So you're going to have chicken breasts for dinner. You could sauté them, grill them or you could make these easy chicken breasts with mushroom sauce. It's just great for a family dinner. Prepare several recipes of it for a dinner party.

5 or 6 boneless skinless chicken breasts
1 Tablespoon White Wine Worcestershire Sauce
1/2 teaspoon of Cajun seasoning (less if you have tender taste buds)
1 4-ounce can of mushroom stems and pieces drained
2 Tablespoons dried parsley
3/4 Cup sour cream or plain yogurt

Place the chicken breasts in an oven proof baking pan. Douse with White Wine Worcestershire Sauce. Sprinkle Cajun seasoning on the chicken, and then scatter the mushrooms over the chicken before dusting with parsley flakes. Bake at 350° for 30 to 35 minutes. This is just enough to cook the chicken and not dry it out.

Remove breasts from pan and set a side for a few seconds leaving the mushrooms and parsley in the pan. Stir the sour cream into the mushrooms and drippings. The residual heat of the pan is enough to warm the sauce. If the sauce is too cool warm gently in the microwave, do not boil the sour cream. It will curdle if you boil it, guaranteed. Pour sauce over the chicken breasts and serve immediately.

Fried Chicken

1 frying chicken, cut up
1½ Cups oil
1 Cup flour
1 Tablespoon Tony's seasoning (Chapter 6)

Cut up the chicken into serving sized pieces. Save the back and neck for stock. In a plastic bag, shake up the flour and seasoning. Preheat the oil in a chicken fryer or heavy skillet. Wash and pat dry the chicken, then place in bag and coat by shaking. Take a pinch of the flour and drop it in the oil to check temperature. If it bubbles, it's hot enough to use. Leaving the oil on high, place chicken parts, skin side down, into the oil, being careful not to splatter the hot oil, and brown thoroughly. As the parts brown, turn over and brown the other side. The white meat pieces will brown more quickly than the dark meat pieces. Reduce heat to medium high, but no lower. This is not a dish that you can walk away from, stay there and pay attention to it. Many home fires are caused by unattended hot oil.

The chicken is thoroughly cooked when browned all the way around, and no blood is oozing from the joints. Remove pieces and place on platter lined with paper towels to absorb the excess oil. Place in 200-225 degree oven to keep warm while making the gravy.

In a heat-proof container, pour off all but 3-4 tablespoons of the oil, keeping the small burnt bits of flour in the pan (drippings) and add 3-4 tablespoons of flour. Follow the directions for making gravy in Chapter 6 and you're set. Serve with sides of mashed potatoes and carrots.

Chicken Roll Ups

   For years I made this dish with chicken thighs. Our sons, Nick and Drew, would eat 4 to 6 thighs apiece. At each place setting, we had surgical scissors for each member of the family to remove the strings from the roll-ups. The boys would eat a few less rolls-up if they had to take the strings off themselves. Of course they would eat a little more rice and vegetables. When Nick and Lisa's twin daughters came home from the hospital, I made up about 20 of the breast roll-ups to help stock the freezer. Just prepare to the point of putting the string on the roll-up, then wrap in plastic wrap and freeze. Thaw as needed and follow the rest of the procedure.

4 boneless skinless chicken breasts or 8 boneless skinless thighs
4 thin slices ham
½ Cup shredded Swiss cheese
½ teaspoon dried thyme leaves
2 to 4 Tablespoons olive oil
¾ Cup dry white wine
¾ Cup sour cream

Flatten chicken breasts with a meat pounder. With smooth side down place a thin slice of ham and one-fourth of the cheese and thyme on the rib side of the breasts. Roll the breast long ways and tie with kitchen string. Preheat a non-stick skillet with olive oil. Brown the roll-up on all sides. Begin with 2 Tablespoons oil, adding more as needed. Pour in wine, cover and steam chicken until tender and cooked through. Remove cover and reduce wine to half the volume. Remove from heat, set chicken aside to rest and remove the string. Stir in sour cream and pour over the chicken breasts. Serve at once. For a smooth sauce, do not boil the sour cream and wine mixture.

Chicken Fried Steak and Gravy

While this recipe is based on beef, we've got it with the chicken recipes purely because of the title. With a little adjustment, the basic recipe can be adapted to a flattened chicken breast, making "Chicken Fried Chicken".

4 minute or beef cube steaks the size of your hand
Salt & pepper
Flour
Oil for frying
1 10-ounce can evaporated milk

Season the flour with salt & pepper. Dredge the cube steaks in the seasoned flour. Fry in oil until golden. Remove from pan and let rest. Drain off all but 2 tablespoons of the fat, keeping all the little brown parts. Stir in ¼ cup flour (this can be the seasoned flour that remains, or fresh), and brown the flour in the fat until lightly browned. Pour in 1 can evaporated milk, bring to boil and then cook for at least a minute. Adjust seasoning, and thin with water if necessary. Serve at once.

Chicken Breast (Glazed with Orange Marmalade)

4 large chicken breasts
Creole seasoning
3 to 4 Tablespoons orange marmalade

Choose chicken breast on the bone with the skin still in place. Sprinkle with Creole Seasoning. Then spread the marmalade over the chicken pieces. Bake in a preheated oven at 350 degree for 35 to 45 minutes.

Coq Au Vin

While living in Louisiana during the 1980's I worked for a while in a department store as the advertising coordinator. A new china & crystal buyer (Carmen) and a new buyer for better women's wear (Domonique who had been a crystal & china buyer before) were hired. I invited both guys to dinner, and we all were seated. Just after the blessing, they both picked up their dinner plates, and inverted them to check the manufacturer! This was the first and only time this had ever happened at my house, but then it was the first time I had ever had two china buyers over for dinner. Fortunately I was using my mother's wedding china, and both men heartily voiced their approval. The following dish comes from Carmen's wife.

¼ pound bacon
Chicken cut up into pieces, or boned chicken thighs
¼ Cup brandy
1 Cup red wine
1 Cup beef broth
2 heaping Tablespoons tomato paste
2 cloves mashed garlic
¼ teaspoon thyme
1 bay leaf

Brown 3-4 ounces bacon and remove. Add 2 tablespoons cooking oil and brown the chicken pieces. Season with salt and pepper, and return bacon to pan, cooking slowly for about 10 minutes. Pour in the brandy and ignite. Then add all the other ingredients, and simmer slowly for about 30 minutes. Take out the chicken and make the sauce, discarding the bacon and bay leaf. Mix 3 tablespoons flour with 2 tablespoons melted butter. Beat this into the cooking liquids. Add 12-24 small cooked onions and ½ pound sautéed mushrooms. Cook and stir until thickened. Pour the sauce over the chicken, and serve with rice or mashed potatoes.

Italian Chicken

This recipe is in our closing/house-warming gift "basket". We have made it hundreds of times over the years with only one memorable failure. Tony put the chicken in the crock-pot and cooked it on high for 12 hours. The sauce was good. The chicken was cooked to shreds of nothing-ness. He said that even the bones seemed a bit soft. The warning here is that all day is way too long, especially on high. This can make any house smell really great. When cooked properly the chicken comes out almost falling off the bone. It's a real meal in itself. Have a Caesar Salad on the side and a bottle of red wine for a special treat. If you make this in a slow cooker, avoid Tony's mistake.

1 whole chicken, cut up
1 jar prepared spaghetti sauce
1 bell pepper, diced
1 medium onion, sliced
1 8-ounce can mushrooms, drained
1 or 2 cloves garlic, crushed
1 Tablespoon basil, crushed
Italian cheese
Salt & pepper to taste
1 4-ounce can tomato paste
1 pound pasta, any kind

Place the first 7 ingredients into a slow cook crock-pot for 4-5 hours, or in a Dutch oven (covered roaster) on low for 2-2 ½ hours. Then, 20-30 minutes before serving, stir in the tomato paste to thicken the sauce and adjust seasoning with salt & pepper. Cook pasta according to package directions.

To serve, pull chicken out of sauce & place on platter. Ladle sauce over pasta. Shake cheese over individual servings.

Cornish Game Hens

This is probably one of the easiest and most fun dishes to prepare, especially when making dinner for a larger group, like for a party or wedding shower. Use the sage dressing recipe (from Pork Chops with Sage Dressing in Chapter 3) and put in an oven-proof baking dish. Plan on half a bird per person, 2 whole birds will fit in a 9x13 inch pan on top of the dressing. With kitchen shears, cut the backbone out and discard. Then split the hens in half with a heavy knife, and place rib side down on top of the unbaked dressing in a pan. Season the birds with Creole seasoning. Bake in 350 degree oven for 45-60 minutes depending on the size of the birds. When the skin is brown and crispy looking, they're done.

For heavier appetites, or variety, you can stuff the birds and stand them up in a baking dish, increase the cooking time to about 1 ¼ hours and you'll have to baste them to keep them from drying out.

Additionally, you could stuff the birds with a rice pilaf. Thoroughly cook the pilaf first, then stuff the birds and bake.

Curry Chicken and Macaroni Salad

Those who truly love curry dishes will probably chuckle at this one. It has a very mild curry taste with a bit of color added to a bland white plate of macaroni. Try it at a luncheon for a group of gals with a couple other salad choices.

12 ounces tri-color spiral pasta (cooked to al dente)
2 Cups roasted chicken boned and cut into pieces
1 Cup frozen baby peas (thaw do not cook) optional
2 ribs celery, chopped
¼ Cup finely minced white onion
¼ Cup pistachio or other nuts

1/3 Cup raisins
1 15-ounce can chunk pineapple drained
1 Cup Mayonnaise (not the "Real" kind, use the whipped)
1 Tablespoon mild curry powder
Salt and black pepper to taste

Mix mayonnaise and curry powder together in small bowl. Mix all other ingredients in large salad bowl. Add dressing and toss. Garnish with green leaf or Romaine lettuce, a sprinkle of coconut, fresh chopped nuts, finely sliced green onions.

Herb Roasted Chicken

Our friend Lyn loves chicken. I have described her as the only person I know who can eat a whole chicken as it crosses the yard and leave the feathers standing. There is nothing delicate about this lady when it comes to chicken. You can also season a whole chicken in the following manner and put it on a smoker for a few hours. Actually, Lyn's husband Doug quite often smokes 3 or 4 birds at once.

4 to 5 pound whole chicken
Tony's Creole Seasoning
Dried thyme

Remove the giblets and neck from the cavity of the bird. Reserve for stock or toss them in the trash. Thoroughly wash the bird inside and out. Pat dry with paper towels. Sprinkle generously with seasoning and thyme.

Place on a gas grill that is preheated to at least 375 degrees. Turn off the side where the chicken will be placed. Adjust the flame on the other side to keep the temperature even, usually around 350. The bird should be perfectly brown and done when the leg wiggles with slight pressure. Use a thermometer to be sure. Remove to a carving board and let rest for 15 minutes.

Poached, Slow Cooked Chicken in White Wine

1 whole chicken
1 medium onion
2 carrots
2 ribs celery
Sprigs of thyme
Sage leaves
2 bay leaves
Salt & pepper
4 ounces fresh mushrooms
1 Cup dry white wine
Can of cream of chicken or asparagus soup

Use a slow cooker. Wash the bird and pat it dry. Put herbs into the cavity. Cut the onion into 16 pieces (1 inch dice). Cut the celery and carrots into 1 inch pieces. Trim mushrooms but leave whole (if they're huge, cut into halves or quarters). Put everything except soup and fresh mushroom into the slow cooker and cook for 4 hours. Add the soup and mushrooms, stirring the soup into the liquid already formed. Then cook 1 more hour. Serve hot. This is really good with brown rice on a cold day.

Pot Pie - Chicken or Turkey

This is another one of those wonderful recipes that answer the question "What do you do with leftovers?" Sometimes we even cook a whole turkey just to have the sliced meat for sandwiches. Whether it's chicken or any other kind of bird, this pot pie recipe is very versatile, and you can make up individual servings or several main course dishes, just depending on what kind of pans you have. This dish freezes extremely well, as long as you keep it sealed from the air.

1 pound boneless skinless cooked chicken or turkey
1 onion
2 ribs celery
Olive oil
4 Tablespoons margarine
6 Tablespoons flour
1 pound mixed frozen vegetables
1 quart poultry stock
1 teaspoon thyme leaves
2 teaspoons parsley
Salt & pepper to taste

The pastry:
1 Cup Crisco
3 Cups flour
1 teaspoon salt
Ice water

Cut chicken into 1 inch pieces and set aside. Dice onion into ¾ to 1-inch dice. Slice celery into ½ inch slices only the green part. Sauté the celery and onions in a bit of olive oil, using large heavy pan such as a Dutch oven. Pour in chicken, stock and vegetables and cook until the green beans are tender. Make a blond roux by melting margarine and stirring in the flour. Spoon into pot mixture to thicken. While the stew is cooking, make the pastry. Cut the shortening into the salt and flour until the texture of corn meal. Add iced water 1-2 Tablespoon at a time until a soft (not crumbly or sticky) dough forms. Divide into 3 pieces, wrap in plastic or wax paper, and chill 10-15 minutes. Roll out pastry the size of thepie pan or oven dish. Ladle thickened stew into the dish, cover with pastry, slit holes in top for steam to escape. Decoratively crimp edges. Freeze or cook immediately in 400 degree oven until it bubbles through crust and crust browns.

The thickened stew may also be poured over biscuits.

Sweet and Sour Chicken

This takes a little time to prep but cooks quickly. Serve with steamed rice. There's enough for four adults. Just make the chicken portion and you've got great chicken nuggets for a real budget price.

1¼ to 1½ pounds chicken thighs (5 to 6)
1 large egg, separated
2 Tablespoons soy sauce
¼ Cup sugar plus ½ teaspoon
¾ teaspoon salt
½ teaspoon black pepper
½ Cup plus 2 Tablespoons cornstarch
½ Cup flour
1 large green pepper
2 medium carrots
1 medium onion
1 medium waxless cucumber
1 small clove of garlic
½ Cup chicken stock
3 Tablespoons rice wine vinegar
2 Tablespoons rice wine
½ Cup water
2 Cups vegetable oil
3 Tablespoons canola or peanut oil
1½ Cups canned pineapple chunks
2 teaspoons sesame oil

Bone and skin the chicken thighs. Cut into 1-inch pieces. Mix egg yolk, 1 tablespoon soy sauce, ½ teaspoon each of sugar, salt and black pepper. Stir in chicken pieces. Sprinkle the chicken with 1 Tablespoon cornstarch. Stir to mix well. Marinate at room temperature for 30 minutes.

Cut green pepper into 1 ¼ inch pieces. Lightly, pound garlic with flat side of clever. Peel and cut carrots into angled slices. Cut onion into 1-inch pieces. Slice cucumber into ¼ inch thick angled slices. Set aside. Drain pineapple. Set aside.

Mix 1 Tablespoon cornstarch with ¼ cup sugar and ¼ teaspoon salt in small bowl. Stir in stock, vinegar, rice wine and 1 Tablespoon soy sauce.

Whisk egg white in medium bowl until foamy and double in volume; whisk in water. Whisk in ½ cup cornstarch until smooth, then ½ cup flour until smooth. Reserve batter.

Heat wok or large fry pan over high heat 20 seconds; add vegetable oil and heat to 350 degrees F. Using 1/3 of chicken pieces at a time, dip each piece in batter and add to wok or pan. Fry until, crisp, golden and cooked through, 4 to 5 minutes. Remove chicken with slotted spoon or drainer. Drain on paper towels. Repeat with balance of chicken in same size batches. Keep temperature at 350 to avoid soggy or heavy fried pieces. Pour off oil and wipe pan clean.

Heat pan or wok over high heat 15 seconds; add 2 Tablespoons canola or peanut oil and heat another 30 seconds. Stir fry green peppers and garlic. Remove from pan discard the garlic. Stir-fry carrots until nearly crisp tender. Keep heat high and add onions and cucumber. Stir-fry until hot and crispy. Remove from pan.

Add 1 Tablespoon oil to pan; heat to hot. Reduce heat to medium. Add drained pineapple; stir-fry 30 seconds. Stir in stock mixture. Increase heat to high, cook and stir until sauce thicken and bubble for 1 minute. Drizzle with sesame oil; stir a couple of times. Return vegetables and chicken to pan. Stir until coated with sauce. Serve immediately.

King Ranch Chicken Casserole

This recipe comes from an Army wife friend. Decades later, while selling real estate in Atlanta, I went to a catered lunch. The agent raved about the deal he got on 2 pans of this casserole, a green salad and a plate of cookies. "What a great deal, only $220." The caterer even threw in a stack of paper plates, some napkins and plastic forks. I think I know who got the real deal.

One package of corn tortillas
1 can cream of chicken soup
1 can cream of mushroom soup
1 can Rotelle brand tomatoes with chilies
1 can mild green chilies
1 chicken (or about 6 large chicken breasts)
8 ounces Colby cheese

Cook chicken and tear into small pieces. The chicken can be poached or roasted. Tear up tortillas into pieces about the size of a 50-cent piece. Mix soups, chilies, and Rotelle brand tomatoes in a separate bowl. Shred the cheese.

Prepare a 9 X 13 pan or other large baking dish by spraying with a no-stick cooking spray or oiling with vegetable oil. Spread a small amount of the soup and tomato mixture on the bottom of the pan. Layer the tortillas, chicken, soup mixture and cheese until pan is full. End with a cheese layer. You should have three layers.

You can now set aside and refrigerate until 45 minutes before serving. If baking directly after layering, cooking time may be reduced. Bake at 350 degrees until bubbly and hot through. Serve with shredded lettuce, chopped tomatoes, sour cream and salsa.

V. Holiday Menus

Looking back, our two tours to the Republic of Korea were the most memorable. The first, when Tony was flying with the Assam Dragons and we lived on Osan Air Base, was our first experience living in a foreign country, and it was a very positive one. The second, when I had a two-bedroom house in Yongsan Army Garrison in Seoul and Tony had a "hooch" at Camp Red Cloud in Ouijongbu, was the most rewarding.

One December we put together one of those slow-cooking dinners and left for a while to do some errands. While we were gone, our quarters on base were vandalized and we caught the would-be robbers red handed. When we returned home, Tony opened the door and we discovered them sitting in the living room in front of the tree. Three young Korean girls, all age 11, had helped themselves to all our Christmas presents underneath the tree, and had ransacked various parts of the house looking for goodies. We got them to sit on the floor in the kitchen while Tony called for the military police. Not really thinking what he was saying, he notified them that he had apprehended three Korean nationals while they were burglarizing our quarters and had them detained in the kitchen. Shortly thereafter, we heard a knock at the door. It was an MP, complete with dog and weapon at the ready. When he saw the three kids, he slowly put his gun away, reached for his radio, and canceled "the rest of the response." Lord only knows how many other armed defenders of Liberty were on their way to rescue the AF pilot who had his hands full with those tough Korean intruders!

I was deeply involved in MWR Services (Morale, Welfare and Recreation), running the on-base closed circuit Television Command Channel, and a variety of public relations programs. The whole family got involved in little theater, with even Tony emerging in his stage debut as "Mac" in "You Cant Take it With You", then as camera and crew in others like "Charley's Aunt", "The Jungle Book", Drew's debut in "The King's Creampuffs", Nick's debut in "Readin, Ritin, and Rithmetic", and Osan's Night of Comedy which presented "Cinderella Wore Combat Boots", "Plaza Suite", and "Lovers and Other Strangers". At one point we expanded it to a dinner theater, with the Recreation Center staff cooking steaks in the parking lot behind the Recreation Center.

Being so far away from home, and so far from the United States stressed to us the need to take every opportunity to build strong family relationships no matter where we were in the world. So we ensured that we preserved the family traditions that we had started. We celebrated the holidays with very predictable meals that we could reproduce nearly anywhere. So no matter what happened during the year, those traditions became stabilizing family events wherever we were. All the holiday meal menus were pretty much etched in stone – occasionally we would try something new on the side, which is how the day after Thanksgiving became the Korean menu.

New Years Day Brunch

The whole idea behind holiday entertaining is to make your guests feel welcome, comfortable and very special. This is my very favorite brunch menu. It's anything but cheap. The very thought of cutting corners during the holidays makes me crazy.

In Real Estate, we always are asked why one property is priced differently than another: "Location, Location, Location!" The same is true with wines: The difference between champagne and sparkling wine is where the stuff is made. Only the sparkling wines from a certain area in France can be called champagne. And it's the law there too! But overall it's simply a matter of taste, and what you like. Similarly, you can't make a dried up Range Hen taste juicy and tender with just a roasting bag (but it helps). Start with quality foods to get the best possible meals.

For the baked ham in this menu, try one of those pre-cooked spiral sliced hams. It looks great and it's easy. Just heat it through and serve. The fruit cup is a great place to use the grapefruit and oranges that you received as a gift. If you don't know how to section a grapefruit so it looks like the sections sold in glass jars at the grocery, check the CD ROM version of this book which shows exactly how to section the fruit.

Since I make this menu for New Years Day, the black-eyed peas are a must-have. We also usually have a supply of headache remedies available for those who stayed up too late the night before.

French Champagne or Sparkling Wine
Baked Ham
Creole Eggs and Shrimp
Quick Caramel Rolls
Fresh Fruit Bowl   Black Eyed Peas
Orange Juice   Fresh Brewed Coffee

Most of this menu can be prepared a day or two ahead of time leaving you plenty of time to be a relaxed hostess.

Quick Caramel Rolls

Here's a recipe that requires assembly the night before the party. But it's easy, tasty and quick, requiring no further work.

24 frozen dinner rolls
1 (3-5/8 ounce) package of butterscotch pudding, **not instant**
½ Cup butter or margarine
¾ Cup brown sugar
1 teaspoon cinnamon
2 teaspoons lemon juice
1 Cup chopped pecans

Butter a large bundt pan. Arrange rolls in pan, sprinkling dry pudding over rolls as you add them. Cook butter and remaining ingredients over low hear until sugar is dissolved and mixture bubbles. Pour over rolls. Cover pan tightly with foil and allow to stand on the countertop overnight. In the morning bake at 350° for 30 minutes. Let stand for 5 minutes, then invert onto a platter. Serves 12-16

Creole Eggs and Shrimp

¼ Cup butter or margarine
1 Cup chopped yellow onion
2/3 Cup chopped green pepper
1 Cup chopped celery
1 Cup sliced fresh mushrooms
1 can cream of mushroom soup
1 can cream of tomato soup
1 Tablespoon chili powder
1 teaspoon Tony Chachere's seasoning (most grocery stores)
1 teaspoon hot sauce
12 hard-boiled eggs
2 Cups grated sharp cheddar cheese

1 pound precooked shrimp
1 Cup Ritz cracker crumbs
1½ Tablespoons Worcestershire sauce

In butter, sauté onions, mushrooms, green pepper and celery. Add soups and seasoning. Simmer until well blended. Sauce will keep several days in the refrigerator, but does not freeze well. On the day of the party boil the eggs, peel and slice. Place in a 3-quart casserole dish that has been greased. Scatter the shrimp over the eggs. Pour the sauce over the eggs and shrimp. Top the casserole with cheese and crumbs. Bake at 450° for 15-25 minutes. Serves 12-16

Sausage Strata

This serves at least 8 people. We have it as part of our New Year's Day Brunch. Even the sleepiest can slide this pan in the oven. Then go shower and dress. When you get back to the kitchen, make a pot of coffee, spoon up some fruit and breakfast is ready.

1 pound bulk pork sausage
10 slices bread
1½ Cups grated Cheddar cheese
6 eggs
2 Cups milk
6 Tablespoon melted butter
1 teaspoon dried mustard

Brown sausage and crumble. Cut bread into 1-inch cubes. Beat eggs to fluffy. Stir in milk, melted butter and mustard. Spray a 9x13 inch pan with a non-stick vegetable oil and add cubed bread. Sprinkle sausage and cheese over the bread. Cover with the egg mixture. Cover, chill over night. Bake at 350 degrees for 40 to 45 minutes. Serve.

Black Eyed Peas

The following recipe is mandatory if you are preparing a New Years Day meal and you are South of the Mason-Dixon Line. Tradition goes you must eat black-eyed peas on New Years Day for good luck. I prefer mine a bit on the spicy side, but by Louisiana guidelines of taste, my peas are a bit bland. This is the part where you need to taste and adjust the seasoning. Remember that you can always add a little more but you can't take the seasoning out if you have overdone it. You might need to re-season and let the peas simmer a couple more minutes two or three times. If you are in Pennsylvania for New Years, make enough for yourself and any southern born guests.

1 pound of dry black-eyed peas
2 Ribs of celery, diced
1 Medium onion, diced
1 Tablespoon minced garlic
2 Tablespoons olive oil
1 large bay leaf
1 teaspoon salt
1 teaspoon Creole seasoning
1 teaspoon liquid smoke

Sort through the peas. Discard any discolored or damaged peas as well as any rocks or clods of dirt. Place in a large bowl and add twice as much water (peas 3-inches deep in the bowl covered with a total of 6-inches of water). The peas will absorb the water. Soak over night or at least 3 or 4 hours. 2 hours prior to service, sauté the celery, onion and garlic until translucent. Drain and rinse the peas. Add to the pot along with 1 inch of water above the peas. Add the bay leaf, salt and ½ the Creole Seasoning. Cook for 1½ to 2 hours until the peas are tender but not mushy. Adjust the taste with the balance of the Creole Season and the liquid smoke. Serve piping hot. This should serve 10 to 15 with the New Years Buffet or 4 hungry people from Louisiana with extra hot sauce and a pan of corn bread.

Black Eyed Peas pg 96

Creole Shrimp & Eggs pg 94

Quick Caramel Rolls pg 94

Turkey pg 98

Setting up a Bar

Whether you are just having a couple of people over for wine and cheese or you giving a cocktail buffet party for 50, setting up the bar prior to the event makes the whole event easier. First decide on the beverages that you are going to serve. Select the glasses appropriate for those drinks. When serving just beer and wine, you don't need martini glasses. However, if you are having a full cocktail buffet, you will probably use most of your crystal, the wine and ice buckets and have an array of olives, cherries, celery and lime wedges on hand as well. When in doubt, ask that friend of yours who tended bar in college. Keep it simple and handy. Do have a cloth for wiping spills, plenty of napkins, sodas, water and juices. Our New Years Day bar includes Champagne, Bloody Marys, soda and juices.

<u>Thanksgiving Dinner</u>

As a child, we had two of each of the holiday dinners. One was at the German grandparents' home. It was always served right at 12 noon. The dressing was bread with sage. The rolls were wonderful and always home baked. The pumpkin and fruit pies were as fresh as the whipped cream that topped them. At about 5 or 6 p.m. there was the French version of the holiday dinner with the other set of grandparents. The turkey was always very moist due to the dressing. Mincemeat pie was always available, however, I don't ever remember eating it. When Tony and I started making our holiday dinners, we added turkey soup made from the wings of the bird and pecan pie. And, we only had one dinner per day.

How to do the turkey: Thaw in the refrigerator. It takes three to five days. Pull out the giblets and refrigerate until you make the broth for the gravy. Take a boning knife and cut out the wings for the soup. Wash the bird with water until clean. Dry well. Place in roasting pan, either stuffed or not. Oil the breast with vegetable oil before baking like putting on baby oil for sunbathing. Bake at 350 degrees in a tented (with foil) pan for 20 minutes per pound if stuffed. Make sure you use a thermometer in the thigh portion and check for doneness. Remove dressing first and put in a bowl. If baking without stuffing, reduce cooking time to about 16 - 18 minutes per pound. While roasting baste every 30 minutes and remove foil tent the last 30 to 45 minutes for browning. Let rest 15 minutes before carving whether stuffed or unstuffed. Do not poke bird with a fork during cooking. It will dry out. Use a Butterball or another self-basting bird for the moistest possible dinner. If using a skinned bird, wrap with bacon to keep it moist.

Make gravy using the drippings from the bird in conjunction with the broth and meat from the giblets. Wing meat is for the soup. Increase flavor with chicken bouillon. Also use salt and pepper.

The trick is getting the bird done without drying it out. If it's a little pink near the bones of the thigh when carving, carve the cooked portion and slide the carcass into the oven at 200 degrees while eating dinner. My secret is to keep it covered, and then let it rest. Amazing how much juice is in a Butterball! Take all the meat off the bones as soon as dinner is over and store in the refrigerator. Freeze the carcass in a plastic bag for soup later.

<u>Meat Dressing</u>

This dressing is probably a version of the French Forced Meat dressing. Of course my French Grandmother was several generations removed from France. Each generation was likely to have made adjustments depending on availability of ingredients and family tastes. This dressing actually adds to the moisture in the bird instead of drying it out.

The most important part of the tradition is that a small portion of the dressing is made into a patty and then pan-fried. This "artery blocker" breakfast is served with a poached egg right after the bird is stuffed. My daughter-in-law skips the egg and has ketchup with her dressing. It's rather amazing that there is enough dressing left to stuff the bird some years.

Or you can stuff a scored and pocketed flank steak with the dressing. Roll and tie with kitchen string. Brown and braise until tender.

Stuff jumbo mushroom caps with the dressing. Place stuffed caps with dressing side up in a shallow baking pan. Pour one-half inch of chicken stock around the caps, about half way up.

Sprinkle with paprika. Bake at 350 degrees until the dressing is browned. Serve one or two with slices of turkey as a very edible garnish or have 3 or 4 as an entrée with a splash of turkey or chicken gravy. The California version substitutes ground turkey for the beef.

To stuff a 12 to 15 pound bird, Brown:
> 1 pound pork sausage
> ½ pound lean ground beef

Add and cook until crisp tender:
> 1 large onion, diced
> 3 or 4 ribs of celery sliced and diced
> ¾ Cup fresh parsley or 1/3 Cup dried

Then add:
> 3 or 4 potatoes mashed (or 4 servings instant potatoes)
> 1/2 stick butter
> 4 eggs beaten
> 1 10½-ounce can evaporated milk
> 1 can chicken broth (add as needed if dressing is too dry or add water. May not be needed when using homemade bread cubes)
> 2 Tablespoons sage rubbed in palms of hands
> 1 big package stuffing bread cubes or small loaf of homemade bread that's been sliced, toasted & diced

Salt and pepper

The dressing should be very moist to almost running with liquid before it is placed in the bird. Fill the turkey cavities with dressing. Do not pack into the bird as you must leave room for expansion. The excess stuffing can be baked separately in covered casserole dish for 45 minutes.

Pecan Pie

This is definitely a simple pie to make. The most difficult part is getting it into the oven without spilling. Serve with a little vanilla ice cream or whipped cream "to cut the sweetness."

1 Cup sugar
1 Cup light corn syrup
4 eggs beaten
1 to 1½ Cup pecan halves or pieces
1½ teaspoons flour
4 Tablespoons melted butter

Beat together adding pecans last. Pour into an unbaked 9-inch pie shell and bake at 350 degrees for about 45 minutes. The middle will rise when it is baked and set. Let cool for at least a couple of hours.

Cranberry Salad

See our great cranberry salad recipe in Chapter 7.

Turkey Breast with Stuffing

Sautee diced onion and celery, season with thyme and sage, plus ½ bag stuffing mix (Pepperidge farm herbed cubed). Add ½ cup chicken broth or more if too dry.

Season breast with thyme and Tony's seasonings (Chapter 6). Cook 17 minutes per pound, or 20 min/pound stuffed, check temperature with a thermometer. About ½ hour before serving, put dressing in oven.

VI. Sauces, Spices & Seasonings

Next on assignment was flying the LDG5-Delta at Langley AFB in Virginia. Tony had gotten orders to be on the staff at what was then Headquarters Tactical Air Command. Egos as they are, whenever someone asked him what he was flying, he would reply "The LGD5-Delta". Some aviators were a little slower on the up-take, so they asked what that was. Proudly Tony would reply, "That's the Large Gray Desk, Five Drawer".

The house we found was on Zilber Court in Hampton, and was located on one of the many tidal rivulets that emptied eventually into the Chesapeake Bay. The view out the back was great, looking out onto protected wetlands, so we were continually entertained with waterfowl and harvesting blue crabs off our dock. We bought our first boat, a flat-bottomed jon boat with a small motor. Once we had gone out to catch dinner, and while returning to the dock, Tony asked me to reach out and grab the dock. Well I did, and ended up pushing rather than pulling, eventually falling fully into the tidal mud and ooze. Unfortunately we had just installed an energy timer on the hot water heater. It was set for hot water only in the morning and late afternoon. I splashed at about 2 p.m. Hence, I got "slimed" and got a cold shower too.

It was here that we really got into seafood, spending a lot of time with our friends in the neighborhood, fishing in the Chesapeake and cooking what we caught. Our favorites were flounder and shark, occasionally punctuated with a bucket full of blue crabs from the traps we set out. Shark wasn't very popular then and the sand sharks were fun to catch, and held together very well when cooked.

We've come a long way from drowning food in sauces to cover up spoiled meat. Prior to refrigeration and preservation advances, a common technique to offset poor tasting food was to prepare a sauce that would overwhelm the offending odors. Today's sauces are present to balance flavors, enhance the dining experience, and to construct complementary bridges from one dish to another. Then of course, there are the pepper sauces and dark roux of Louisiana that stand up and say "Good Morning" with most any food.

Blue Cheese Salad Dressing

When I worked for the first time in a restaurant, I was amazed at some of the extenders that were used. The head chef would stir a quart of small curd cottage cheese into a gallon of prepared blue cheese dressing to make it look like it had more chunks of cheese in it. The whipped butter was actually half butter and half margarine and was whipped in a huge mixer until it had so much air in it that it was almost white. The whipped "butter" was then chilled and scooped with a small ice cream type scoop. It melts quickly on warm rolls and that's what the patrons wanted. Notice this dressing has no cottage cheese in it. It's a savory blend that will make bottled dressing a thing of the past.

4 ounces crumbled blue cheese
2 Cups of your favorite mayonnaise
2 Cups buttermilk
Juice of half a lemon

Mix all ingredients together and "age" 24 hours in the refrigerator. This dressing will keep for a week or so.

Australian Mint Sauce

(Thanks to Penelope's mum in Australia for this one)

5 garlic cloves
A bunch mint leaves, around 12
2 Tablespoons brown sugar
1 Tablespoon kosher salt
2 teaspoons black pepper
2 Tablespoons Canola oil

Puree. Serve on the side with a good leg of Australian lamb

Barbecue Dry Rub

This is a great rub for chicken or ribs. Put it on thick if you like spicy food, sparingly if you want just a hint of taste. The rub helps keep the juices in, especially if you like skinning your chicken before cooking. This works great for adding a little flavoring to chicken.

¼ Cup paprika
2 Tablespoons granulated garlic
2 Tablespoons granulated onion
2 teaspoons peppercorns
1 teaspoon dry mustard
1 teaspoon chili powder
2 Tablespoons cumin seed, toasted
3 Tablespoons coriander seed, toasted
¼ Cup kosher salt
¼ Cup light brown sugar
1 whole chicken, cut in pieces

Grind all ingredients in a clean coffee grinder until well mixed. Rub on chicken directly or coat in a plastic storage bag. Make sure chicken is dry before applying. Or just sprinkle a little over the chicken lightly, like salt and peppering it.

Basil Cubes

(Or, how to preserve your herb garden over winter)

Harvest your crop of basil, and strip all the leaves off the stems. Wash thoroughly and toss a few handfuls into a food processor with a little water. Process until all the leaves have been ground up, but still leaving small chunks. Keep it moist by adding water as necessary. Scoop out and/or pour into ice cube trays, ensuring an even amount of puree and liquid. If they are too dry they will not freeze. Freeze thoroughly. Pop them out and into a freezer bag for better storage. One cube thawed and drained equals one Tablespoon of chopped fresh basil.

Blackening

Originally based on a Cajun recipe, we've adjusted the ingredients here to cool it down a lot from the Louisiana version. Our friend Doug, who has tried to teach Tony how to bass fish for years, would triple the onion, garlic and cayenne! Use this on anything you're going to blacken: fish, beef, pork, more fish, etc. The secret is to keep the skillet very, very hot so that it sears the blackening and keeps the juices inside without charring.

1 Tablespoon paprika
¼ teaspoon salt
1 teaspoon onion powder
1 teaspoon garlic powder
Pinch ground red pepper
½ teaspoon dried thyme leaves
½ teaspoon dried oregano leaves

Using fish steaks no greater than ¾ inch thick, dip fish into melted butter, then sprinkle seasoning and pat it on. Put fish on HOT skillet (white hot iron skillet is best, hot enough to vaporize a drop of butter), and then pour 1Tablespoon butter over the fish (it WILL flare up!!!) Cook until charred about 2 min. Flip over and repeat. Key to this recipe is keeping the skillet super hot.

Butters

The use of flavored butters can enhance most meals. The savory ones give a zing to meats and vegetables. Use sweet fruit butters with breads, muffins and pancakes. Form the butter into rolls wrapped in plastic wrap then in foil. Freeze until ready to use. Slice into thick pat while butter is still frozen or very firm.

Savory Butters

Soften one stick or ¼ pound salted butter. Stir in 1/3 of a cup of finely minced fresh herbs. Try chives, rosemary, mint, sage, or parsley. Any of these will partner well with garlic. Use 4 large cubes that have been minced. The herbs can be used with meats or vegetables. Mint, butter and peas make a good match. Sage butter will partner well with pork or chicken. Use your imagination.

Fruited Butters

Soften one stick or ¼ pound salted butter. Stir-in 1/3 cup of dried fruit or fresh berries. Chopped raisins, dates, currants, dried cranberries, cherries or other dried fruits work well. Use fresh firm berries like blueberries and raspberries. Apricots and other firm drier fruits should be finely chopped.

Mint and Garlic Butter

¼ pound softened butter
4 cloves minced garlic
½ Cup fresh mint leaves

Whip the softened butter with electric mixer. Mix in the finely sliced mint leaves and garlic. Form into a log on a piece of plastic wrap or waxed paper. Chill in freezer until firm. Slice medallions and set out, or leave in freezer wrapped in wax paper until needed.

Cranberry Amaretto Chutney

(Serves 4 to 6)
2 Cups cranberries
1 Cup sugar
1 Tablespoon lemon juice
1 Tablespoon Orange marmalade
½ teaspoon lemon zest
¼ Cup Amaretto (or 1 miniature bottle)

Combine cranberries, sugar and lemon juice in small saucepan. Cook over medium heat, stirring constantly until mixture comes to a boil. No additional liquid is needed. Reduce heat and simmer 20 minutes. Remove from heat, stirring in lemon zest, amaretto & marmalade. Stir until blended. Refrigerate and use over cream cheese with crackers or with fowl or pork. To seal in jars: sterilize jars and lids, pour bubbling mixture into jars while still hot. Clean rim, add lid and ring, secure tightly. The jars will seal as they cool. Keep without refrigeration until opened.

Kara's Microwave Hollandaise Sauce

Good recipes come from people of all ages. Our friend's daughter, Kara was about 13 when she shared this one with us.

1/3 Cup melted butter
2 beaten egg yolks
2 Tablespoons fresh lemon juice
Pinch of salt

Melt the butter in the microwave. Add egg yolks, fresh lemon juice and pinch of salt. Microwave on high for 30 seconds. Whisk until smooth. Microwave in 15-second stages, whisk after each stage until smooth for a total of one minute. Sauce will thicken as it sits.

Salad Dressing Mix

Doris Giacobe, my mother-in-law, was one of the kindest and most thoughtful people I have ever met. A great cook she was not, hence very, very few of her recipes have survived. She could make a great baked fish and had this recipe for salad dressing. It's light and spicy, and a good start for experimenting with your own flavors.

4 Tablespoons salt
1 Tablespoon minced dried garlic
4 Tablespoons minced dried onions
1 Tablespoon black pepper
1 Tablespoon sugar
1 Tablespoon paprika

Mix all the dry ingredients and keep sealed until needed. Use 2 tablespoons of mix with ¼ cup cider or wine vinegar and 2/3 cup salad oil. Put in a bottle and shake. Refrigerate 24 hours before using. Using olive oil or part olive oil can vary flavor in the dressing. Adding more vinegar will give a sharper taste.

Tony's Seasoning

1 (26 ounce) box Morton's salt
1½ ounces ground pepper
2 ounces ground red pepper (cayenne)
1 ounce garlic powder
1 ounce MSG (Accent)
1 ounce chili powder

Mix thoroughly. Makes enough for 2 quart jar.

Elderflower Cordial

The elderberry plant grows domesticated or wild alongside roadways and open fields, and the flowers and berries can be used in cooking. This is a very pleasant non-alcoholic afternoon sipping concoction that can take the place of lemonade on a warm day. Thanks to our dear friend Jenny in England. Gather the elderflowers yourself and ensure you de-bug them completely.

1 liter water
1 Kg sugar
Large juicy lemons sliced
3 teaspoons citric acid
About 40 heads of elderflowers
1 teaspoon sodium meta bisulphate (Camden tablet or whatever your equivalent used in wine making).

Dissolve water and sugar, then add lemons, citric acid and elderflower heads, and bring to boil for about 3 minutes. Leave to stand for several hours. Drip through jelly bag and add sulfite or Camden tablet. Bottle in sterile/clean bottles. Mix ¼ cup of the cordial with 1 liter sparkling water. Happy drinking!

Pepper Jelly - Hot

½ Cup hot peppers (red & green)
1½ Cups green bell peppers
1½ Cups vinegar
6½ Cups sugar
1 or 2 pouches Certo
1/8 teaspoon red or green food coloring
6 or 7 half pint jars

Remove seeds and veins from peppers (wear rubber gloves when working with hot peppers). Chop some and grind in food processor or blender. You may use some of the vinegar with the peppers when grinding. In large pot, mix all ingredients except Certo and food coloring; bring to rolling boil and boil for 5 minutes. Add Certo and boil for 1 minute. Remove from heat and let stand 5 minutes. Skim if necessary and add food coloring. Put in jars and seal. Turn upside down for a while to keep bits of peppers from rising to the top. Yields 6 to 7 half pints

Spinach Walnut Pesto

Sometimes you meet a person and know that you will be friends. Susan was like that. She had a great haircut and when we first met I asked who cut her hair. It took another year and a half until she gave up the person's name and location. But that was only after I got a haircut so bad it looked like I had been cutting my own hair without a mirror or sharp scissors.

¾ Cup walnuts
1 (10 ounce) bag fresh spinach, washed and pan-seared to tender
¼ Cup olive oil
1 Tablespoon chopped garlic
½ teaspoon salt
½ teaspoon pepper
¾ Cup grated Parmesan cheese

Preheat oven to 300 degrees and lightly toast the walnuts on a baking sheet for 7 minutes. Let cool. Whip the nuts in a processor until fine. Remove to a bowl. Put in the spinach, oil, garlic salt and pepper and whiz until just smooth. Add the cheese and nuts and whiz just to combine. To serve, toss with hot cooked pasta over low heat. Add a little stock or water if the sauce is too thick to combine evenly with the pasta. The pesto can be covered with a thin layer of olive oil and stored in the refrigerator or freezer.

Roux, Sauces, and Gravy

A roux is the first step toward making a sauce that you don't want to thicken later with cornstarch. A roux is flour where each granule of flour is coated with fat so that when it is mixed with liquid, it doesn't form lumps. Each granule expands on its own when surrounded with fat, rather than attaching to other flour granules and making lumps. There is brown roux and there is blond roux. A blond roux is made with butter and flour, while a brown roux is made with oil or lard that can stand high temperatures. Usually you use equal amounts of flour and fat. Melt the butter and cook with flour for about a minute, mixing as you go so that each granule is coated. Once completely mixed, you can then add your other ingredients to make your sauce.

Using a white roux (2 Tablespoons butter plus 2 Tablespoons flour), add 1 Cup milk to make a béchamel sauce, or a medium white sauce. 1Tablespoon flour plus 1 Tablespoon butter and 1 cup milk is a thin white sauce used to thicken soup. 3 Tablespoons flour plus 3 Tablespoons butter and 1 Cup milk is a thick white sauce used for a binder with meats to make things like croquettes.

The brown roux is cooked over slow to medium heat until the roux turns a deep color like chocolate. Be careful not to burn it. If you do , throw it away and start over. Use a Brown roux to thicken soups, make meat gravies, and so on. If you're a Cajun, make a big batch and save it in the fridge, for use as you go. In Louisiana, they say "if you're gonna make roux, put the baby down to sleep, put a lock on the front door, and take the telephone off the hook, cause you can't be disturbed." For a good brown roux, start with a cup of flour and a cup of fat.

Gravy

The slurry method is done by dissolving flour or cornstarch in water. When using cornstarch, use half as much as you would if using flour, because it has twice the thickening power as flour. To make the slurry, start with a cup of water and a ¼ Cup of flour. Whisk or shake together in a tightly closed jar. After deglazing a pan, pour in the slurry and have additional liquid on the side. Mix the slurry with the pan drippings stirring as you go. It will thicken as you heat it. Add additionally liquid like the carrot or potato water to add additional flavor and to thin the gravy, or add more flour/water mixture to thicken. Never use water that has boiled any cabbage family vegetables as it is too strongly flavored. Taste, and adjust the seasoning as needed. If the gravy has no taste it usually needs salt or herbs. Use black pepper sparingly.

Another way to make gravy is to make a roux using the fat and pan drippings from your main course. Sprinkle 1-2 Tablespoons flour into the bottom of the pan, stir with wooden spoon to ensure all the flour has been coated with fat, cook for a minute or two, then add about 1 cup liquid. Again, season to taste. This method is the chanciest, meaning the one that is most likely to produce lumps.

Vinegars with Herbs

These herbed vinegars make great gifts. Use the vinegar on a salad or as a base for a salad dressing. The cranberry is very tart. Prepare all your ingredients and ensure jars are washed properly (we use clear wine bottles). Sealing is important: we cork the wine bottles, but you can plug, or cap yours. A final touch is to seal the corks with colored wax. When selecting ingredients for the vinegar, remember that the vinegar will change the color of the fruit or herbs. Fresh green basil does not work well as it turns out a muddy olive drab.

Rosemary Pepper Vinegar

2-3 pieces plain rosemary
3 red cayenne peppers
Boiling cider vinegar – enough to fill bottles

Rosemary Garlic Vinegar

2-3 pieces plain rosemary
3 cloves garlic
Boiling cider or distilled vinegar – enough to fill bottles

Purple Basil Vinegar

Bunch of dried purple basil. Steep in distilled white vinegar
Wash fresh purple basil and add to the bottle. Remove steeped
basil when it has given up its color and discard. Add colored
vinegar to bottles

Cranberry Vinegar

1 pound fresh cranberries
2 gallon cider vinegar

Steep the cranberries in 1 gallon of the vinegar to color and
flavor. The cranberries will become almost white. Strain out the
spent berries. String fresh berries on wooden sticks. Place in
bottles, add hot vinegar to bottles, filling halfway up. Heat a gallon
of cider vinegar and top off. Makes 10 fifths.

Vinegar Pepper Sauce

Fill your bottle with as many hot peppers as you care to.
Pour hot vinegar to top off. Let sit capped several days and tap the
bottle to release air. Top off with vinegar and seal. This is very
similar to Tabasco pepper sauce.

Other ideas: garlic chive, blueberry, garlic, or thyme.

VII. Sides and Salads

We went back to Louisiana and the A-10 and we got heavily involved with our son Drew's swim team. Like any kids sports, this took a lot of time and the team traveled all over the state for different swim meets. During the week in the summer, Drew would go to morning practice and then their group would descend on our house for breakfast. The six of them would inhale a couple large boxes of cereal while they were cooking the pancakes (we quickly learned how to make pancake mix from scratch). This was also the summer that we bought 3 cases of chicken (66 birds) and cut them up for the freezer, just to stay ahead of the swim team. We also developed a couple really neat recipes: Chicken and Sausage Gumbo (see Soups) and the Cowboy Cookies became Swimmers Bars (see Desserts).

One year around Christmas time, we were out visiting one of our friends on base, in fact I think we were helping them put in an icemaker. Well, we got a phone call from Nick who said that the icemaker line in our attic had burst from the extremely cold temperatures, and that it was raining in the kitchen. He said that he had already shut off the main water line, and that he had the problem "contained." We told him we were on the way, and quickly hung up and headed home. We knew that all of his

training in JROTC (Junior Reserve Officer Training Corps) and Scouting had come into play, and that the situation was well in hand. What worried us most was his use of the phrase "contained". You see, in Navy JROTC, their fire training course stressed containing fires aboard ship by using an ax to cut huge holes in the side of the ship to ventilate and move water around from compartment to compartment. We arrived to find that he had indeed contained the problem, using towels to form a dam, containing the water in the kitchen area alone.

In August 1990 Iraq invaded Kuwait, and Tony and the Flying Tigers went off to Saudi Arabia for a few months as the buildup for Operation Desert Storm got into full swing. He was the first man on the ground from the 74th. Landing at King Fahd international airport was interesting to say the least, since the airport was still under construction and not yet operational. The buildup brought contractors in to provide meals at a make-shift mess hall - camel with fries was a popular meal, in fact the only meal for a long time. Eventually they were able to round out the menu with other offerings, side dishes, fresh salads, and other entrees including chicken and a wide variety of fresh vegetables.

Bread & Butter Pickles

If you grow cucumbers, these pickles are a great way to preserve the summer all year round. They also make great gifts for those friends and neighbors at Christmas. Our Korean housekeeper called them "American Kimchi."

12 cucumbers sliced
6 onions
½ Cup Salt
2 Cup vinegar
2 Cups sugar
1 teaspoon mustard seed
1 teaspoon turmeric

3 teaspoons cornstarch
1 teaspoon celery seed
1 scant teaspoon black pepper
1 teaspoon ground ginger

Soak cucumbers and onions in salt and enough water to cover for about an hour. Mix all the rest together and bring to a boil for 1 minute. Add drained onions and cucumbers, mixing gently and heat thoroughly, but do not boil. Pack in jars and seal: if mixture is still warm enough, jars will seal when they cool. If not, then hot process. Ready in 4-6 weeks.

Watermelon Rind Pickles

There are some recipes that you make and enjoy but don't make again for years. Then you make the recipe again and remember why. For me, it took 20 years between preparation of this very sweet and very crisp treat. It's a lot of work.

Select watermelon with thick rind. Peel and cut watermelon rind into strips approximately one inch wide. Cut strips into about one inch pieces, or larger if desired. Be sure to cut off all red meat. You should have one gallon of rind.

Mix two Cups pickling lime with two gallons water. Pour lime water over rind and let stand for twelve hours. Use crockery ware, porcelain or glass containers for your product. Remove rind from lime water. Soak in fresh cool water for two hours. Wash in fresh water three times. Cook in clear water until transparent. Remove from heat and drain well.

For syrup:
5 Cups sugar
6 teaspoons mixed spices (tied in cloth bag)
3 pints white vinegar

Bring to hard boil and add red or green cake coloring. Add to well-drained rind and cook another five or ten minutes. Pour into clean hot jars and seal.

Pickled Green Tomatoes

When we have grown tomatoes, there is always a glut of fruit just before the first frost takes the plants. This recipe takes care of all those tomatoes with a very tasty outcome. Green cherry tomatoes are really easy to get into the jars.

8 hot peppers
16 cloves garlic
1 box dill seed
1 box pickling spice
2 gallons green tomatoes, small
2 quarts vinegar
2 quarts water
1 Cup salt

Place green tomatoes whole in jars. Put in each jar: 1 hot pepper, 2 cloves garlic, 2 teaspoons dill seed, 1 teaspoon pickling spice. Boil vinegar water and salt. Pour over tomatoes and seal. Ready in 6 weeks. Okra can be used in place of the tomatoes. If too hot, delete the hot pepper and 1-garlic clove, and halve the pickling spice.

Bean Salad

This is a staple of summer picnics and church suppers in the Midwest. There are no eggs to spoil in this or the carrot salad. I thought it was a special treat because my father hated beans, so we rarely ate them at home. Put this salad next to the Copper Pennies and a potato salad and you have a colorful salad bar for sure.

1 can cut green beans
1 can yellow wax beans
1 can dark red kidney beans
½ Cup minced onion
½ Cup diced green bell pepper
½ Cup Canola oil
½ Cup white vinegar

¾ Cup sugar
1 teaspoon salt
½ teaspoon pepper

Drain the beans. Rinse the kidney beans. Combine beans, onion, and bell pepper in a mixing bowl. Combine remaining ingredients in a blender and process until well combined. Pour liquid over beans and toss carefully. Let stand in refrigerator at least overnight to chill and marinate. Toss daily until used. Keeps a week or more refrigerated. Drain with slotted spoon to serve.

Calico Beans

8 slices of bacon
½ medium yellow onion, diced
2 16-ounce cans pork and beans, keep the juice
1 15-ounce can each of 5 other beans e.g.: black beans, pinto beans, baby lima, butter beans, black-eyed peas, dark red kidney beans…. Drain and rinse all
¾ Cup brown sugar
¾ Cup ketchup
2 teaspoons mustard
1 ½ Tablespoons Worcestershire Sauce
½ large green bell pepper, diced
½ large red bell pepper, diced
½ large yellow bell pepper, diced

Fry bacon until crisp. Remove and reserve to crumb into dish later. Pour off most of the bacon drippings leaving the browned bits and 1 to 2 Tablespoons of bacon fat. Sauté bell peppers and onions in the drippings. Drain. In a very large oven proof casserole stir together the pork and beans with its juice and all the other drained beans. Stir in thoroughly all other ingredients with the exception of the bacon. Sprinkle crumbled bacon over the top and stir in lightly. Bake at 350 degrees for 45 minutes until the whole dish is bubbling. Serve with other buffet items. This dish is dense and will hold temperature for an hour or more.

Cindy's Party Potatoes

When my friend Cindy cooks, she refers to the written recipe, always. She makes some dishes a couple times a month and each time she does, she pulls out the recipe. Of course, her dishes always turn out the same, which says a lot for referring to the recipe. A stand mixer is a great help for this dish.

1/3 Cup butter
4 Cup hot mashed potatoes
1 8-ounce package cream cheese
¼ Cup sour cream
½ teaspoon salt
¼ teaspoon pepper
Paprika to taste

Mix all together and serve. Will hold a long time in the oven.

Marinated Green Bean Salad

1 pound fresh green beans
1 large red bell pepper
½ Cup Wishbone Robusto Italian Salad Dressing
¼ Cup balsamic vinegar

Trim the beans, cook until crisp tender. Drain. Shock in cold ice water. Slice the peppers, drain the chilled beans, and place in airtight container. Pour salad dressing and balsamic over the vegetables, and marinate overnight. Keeps up to a week .

Copper Penny Salad

My best friend Cindy introduced me to these golden jewels. There's just enough crunch, a hint of sweetness and a bit of tang. Since Warner, Cindy's husband, would never consider consuming these treats, we have them whenever the girls get together. If you make half the vegetables, use only half the marinade. Chill the other half in a spill proof container. It makes a tasty red French dressing.

2 pounds thinly sliced carrots, cooked to crisp-tender drained, chilled in ice water bath.
½ small purple onion diced
1 large bell pepper diced

Marinade:
        1 can tomato soup
        1/2 Cup vegetable oil
        1/2 Cup vinegar
        1/2 Cup sugar
        1 teaspoon dry mustard
        1/2 teaspoon ground black pepper

Put the marinade ingredients in blender. Blend until smooth. Pour over vegetables and marinade at least 24 hours. Keeps up to 2 weeks in the refrigerator. Drain with a slotted spoon before serving.

Garlic Mashed Potatoes

Boil some red skinned potatoes until fork tender and drain. Add 1 Tablespoon minced garlic, using electric hand mixer, whip until fairly smooth. Season with salt and pepper, and beat in 3-4 Tablespoons butter, and enough evaporated milk to achieve desired consistency. Remember the potatoes should be thicker than the gravy.

Regular Mashed Potatoes

Peel the potatoes first, and omit the garlic. Remember, don't make it so smooth that they'll think it's instant – leave a few lumps for texture.

Herbed Sliced Potatoes

1 large thin skinned baking potato
½ teaspoon dried thyme leaves
2 teaspoons dried parsley
1`/4 teaspoon garlic powder
½ teaspoon salt
1/8 teaspoon black pepper
1 teaspoon melted butter
1 Tablespoon grated Parmesan cheese

Scrub the potato and dry. Cut 1/8 inch slices almost through the potato, leaving 1/8 of the potato at the bottom intact by placing chopsticks or wooden skewers on either side of the potato as you cut. Combine the next five ingredients and sprinkle over the potato. Drizzle with melted butter and dust with cheese. If thin skinned potatoes are not available, peel the potatoes.

Herbed Red Skin Potatoes

8 –10 small red potatoes
1 teaspoon fresh thyme leaves, minced
1 Tablespoon fresh parsley, chopped
1 teaspoon fresh dill weed, minced
1 Tablespoon fresh chives, snipped
2 Tablespoons butter
Salt & pepper

Wash potatoes and peel a strip around the outside of each. Boil and reduce to simmer, cooking until fork-tender. Drain and return to sauce pan. Toss potatoes, herbs and butter together. Season with salt and pepper. Serve at once.

Potato Salad

There are probably as many ways to make a potato salad, as there are cooks who make it. I have eaten many versions of German style potato salad, French style made with no mayonnaise, and even a mashed potato salad. The all-time worst was a salad made with potatoes that weren't cooked enough at some long forgotten restaurant.

2 to 3 pounds small red potatoes
1/3 Cup minced onion
2 ribs of celery, chopped
4 hard cooked eggs, chopped
2 teaspoons Worcestershire Sauce
2 Tablespoons salad mustard
1 Cup Miracle Whip
Salt and Pepper
2 hard cooked eggs, sliced
Paprika

Cook potatoes until tender. Pour off water and cool. Slip the skins from the potatoes and discard the skins. Slice the potatoes into a large bowl. Sprinkle the onion, celery and chopped eggs over the potatoes and toss lightly. Mix Worcestershire sauce, mustard, and Miracle Whip together in a small bowl. Season with salt and pepper. Add the sauce to the potato mixture. Stir together. Do this carefully, the potatoes should hold their shape and not become mush. Transfer to serving bowl. Decorate with eggs and Paprika. If the salad seems dry, use more Miracle Whip prior to decoration.

Sweet & Sour Green Beans

The first time I cooked on television was at KALB-TV in Alexandria, Louisiana. Ethma Odum was the popular host of a local daily talk program. There were probably five or six times that we cooked together. During the height of beans coming from the garden I shared this recipe with all of Central Louisiana.

1 pound green beans
1 small onion chopped
3 slices bacon
3 Tablespoons brown sugar
3 Tablespoons vinegar

Cook the beans and onion together and drain. Fry the bacon to crisp, remove from pan and pat dry. Add brown sugar and vinegar to the drippings in the pan and heat up. Pour over beans and then crumble the bacon into bits over the top.

Sautéed Chicken Livers

When your best friend gets braces on her teeth a few days before Christmas, you make something she likes and can chew. That Christmas, Cindy ate chicken livers, soup, mashed potatoes, and pumpkin pie. Years later she told me that she just didn't eat most of the time when she had braces because it was so hard to clean her teeth and they hurt a lot too.

1 pound chicken livers
All purpose flour
Salt
Pepper
Vegetable oil
Dry white wine
Water

Rinse chicken livers, drain in a sieve. Remove excess moisture by placing on several layers of paper towel. Dredge in flour seasoned with salt in pepper. In a shallow skillet heat ½ to ¾ inches of vegetable oil. Drop individual livers into hot oil and sauté until browned. Remove to a rack to drain. Continue to fry livers in the oil until all have been browned. Drain oil from the pan. Deglaze the pan with 2 or 3 Tablespoons of dry white wine. Put the livers back in the pan. Add ¼ to 1/3 Cups of water. Bring liquid to a boil and let livers steam with the pan covered. The livers will finish cooking and a nice sauce will form.

Tomatoes a la Ernst

Our friend Vince was a former Marine Pilot, father of four girls, and general character who was a good neighbor of Tony's parents. He served this dish with roasted leg of lamb or beef roast. This is a nice colorful dish that adds dimension to any gathering. He had a "special code" that he used with his family to describe anything that he really didn't like the taste of. He'd describe it as "tasty." If it was really bad, he'd say it was "really tasty."

2 one pound cans whole tomatoes
1 teaspoon Italian herbs (mixture of oregano, basil, rosemary, etc.)
¼ teaspoon garlic powder
1 teaspoon sugar
2 to 3 drops red food color (optional)
1 Tablespoon cornstarch
Salt and Pepper
¼ Cup Parmesan cheese

Drain one can of tomatoes, drain and reserve the other can of juice. Mix reserved juice of 1 can of tomatoes with cornstarch, sugar, herbs, food color, garlic powder and salt and pepper. Arrange tomatoes in baking pan; pour juice mixture over the tomatoes.

Bake 325-350 degrees for 30 minutes or longer, to be timed with rest of meal. Sprinkle with grated cheese (parmesan) and put under broiler until cheese runs.

Cranberries and Apples for Pork

This is a great side dish with any pork entrée like chops, a roast, or pork steaks. The color is vibrant. The flavor can be sweeter or more piquant by simply adjusting the amount of brown sugar.

¼ Cup butter
2 Cups cored fresh apples
2 Cups fresh or frozen cranberries
½ Cup brown sugar
Juice of ½ a lemon

Melt butter in a large sauté pan. Slice apples and sauté for a couple of minutes. Add cranberries and brown sugar. Cook until the berries pop and a thick syrup develops. Add the lemon and serve hot.

Stuffed Tomatoes (Hot)

1 medium onion, finely chopped
1 pound lean (90%) ground beef
4 jumbo ripe tomatoes (about 14 ounces each)
1 Cup loosely packed fresh mint leaves
½ Cup uncooked instant white rice
or ¾ Cup leftover cooked rice

In nonstick 12-inch skillet, cook onion and ground beef over medium-high heat 10 minutes or until meat is browned, breaking up meat with side of spoon.

Meanwhile, cut thin slice from stem end of each tomato; reserve. With spoon, scoop out seeds and pulp from each tomato; reserve. Transfer shells to microwave-safe plate and cook in microwave oven on High 2 minutes or just until heated through. Chop mint and reserved tomato slices and pulp.

Stir chopped tomatoes, rice, 1¼ teaspoons salt, and ¼ teaspoon ground black pepper into meat mixture. Cover and cook 10 minutes. Stir in mint. Fill tomato shells with meat mixture.

Fried Zucchini, Italian Style

Squash, the vegetable not the game, will bring a smile or a grimace to most faces. There seems to be no middle ground. Tony will eat this dish as long as the zucchini are very well browned, seasoned and more than heavily dusted with Italian cheese. Personally, I prefer the dish a little more to the crisp tender side with the zucchini sliced a bit thicker. Try adding yellow summer squash for a bit of color variation or a couple of seeded plum tomatoes and a quarter of an onion sliced.

1 Tablespoon olive oil
3 to 4 fresh dark green zucchini, sliced
2-4 ounces sliced fresh mushrooms
Salt and pepper
Fresh shredded Romano or Parmesan cheese

Preheat a non-stick sauté pan with the olive oil. Place the zucchini and mushrooms in a single layer in the hot pan. Brown. Toss and brown the other side. Shred cheese over the squash and continue to cook until cheese begins to melt.

Cranberry Salad

Two times in my life I have forgotten the sugar in a recipe. The first was a Thanksgiving back when we lived in Austin, circa 1978 or 79. It was in this salad. Yes, there was pucker power that day. The second omission was with pumpkin pie on Thanksgiving 1995. The pie was such a bright orange. My niece wouldn't eat it and my brother-in-law who also had a piece of the pie didn't say a thing about it. Solve the problem by measuring out all the ingredients before starting. And do it in order of assembly.

This particular recipe makes a lot. Consider making just half a recipe unless you're going to feed the whole congregation at the local church supper.

1 pound fresh cranberries
1 large orange, seeded
1 large crisp apple seeded and cored
2 Cups sugar
2 packages red cherry Jell-O
1 Cup pecan pieces
1 Cup chopped celery
2 Cups boiling water

Grind cranberries, orange skin and all, as well as apple skin and all. Dissolve Jell-O in water. Pour sugar over fruit and stir well. Add Jell-O to fruit, stir in nuts and celery. Pour into two 9 inch by 13 inch pans and chill until firm. Makes too much. Unless you're serving 20 people, cut recipe in half. Serve squares on plates lined with lettuce leaves. Top with dab of sour cream.

Fruit Bowl

Making a fruit bowl depends on what you like, and what is available, balancing sizes, colors and the size of your bowl. A winter fruit bowl will look much different from a summer one. When we lived in Asia, we always included Asian Pear-Apples in the fall and winter, and strawberries in the spring. Do not use fresh cranberries or gooseberries. They are much too tart.

Apples	Grapes
Grapefruit	Pears
Oranges	Bananas

A rule of thumb is to use one piece of fruit for each person. Section the citrus fruit and cut the apples, pears and bananas into large bite sized pieces. Do the citrus first and then drop in the apples and pears so that the acid from the citrus keeps the other fruit from turning dark. Layer in a clear glass bowl. Add the bananas at the last moment. They turn dark no matter what you do. This can be done the day before the party adding the banana as described.

Basil Cubes pg 106

Copper Penny Salad pg 121

Marinated Green Bean Salad pg 120

Herbed Vinegars pg 113

Bean Soup pg 134

Chili pg 133

Onion Soup pg 135

Pumpkin Cubes for Soup pg 131

VIII. Soups

In February 1991, we moved to Fort Riley, occupying temporary quarters for six months before moving to permanent quarters in 89A Schofield Circle, facing the Artillery Parade field. Quarters 89 was constructed in 1905 in the Pond/Jacobs era, and measured approximately 5500 square feet on our side of the common wall, with unfinished basement and a finished third floor. It was so spacious that we had to install a four station intercom system just to find each other. It, like many of the other historically registered buildings, was constructed of limestone block that had been originally quarried from one of the five nearby stone quarries. Since the stone itself was of a soft nature, it was prone to the mechanical action of organic growth in the summer and freezing water in the winter. The 12 foot ceilings and four working fireplaces gave the structure an impressive appearance, but "105" and "155" howitzer firings on the nearby ranges continuously rattled the windows. Fluffy, our longhair Persian cat, quickly learned the difference between cannon fire and thunder. She also took a liking to "hunting" the plethora of squirrels we had through the tall and many windows of our quarters.

Tony commanded a 52 person Tactical Air Control Party, a command and control unit for close air support aircraft. As the

division's Air Liaison Officer, he provided direct advice on the use of airpower to the commanding general and staff of the First Infantry Division, Mechanized, "The Big Red One." This assignment was to be the first of our three close experiences with the Army. It also introduced us to several interesting menus and dishes not previously experienced.

One of the battalion commanders was very, very Scottish, and when he threw a St Andrews Day party, we got to sample the famous "haggis". Then one summer we cooked an entire pig and had Tony's squadron over for the picnic. We also began our yearly Thanksgiving celebrations with friends Ed and Suzy. The gourmet club at Fort Riley also afforded us the opportunity to investigate our Italian cooking roots and re-discovered Minestrone and a variety of chicken based soups.

Later, while selling new homes, I found a way to keep prospects in the house talking just a little bit longer. Just make the house smell good. The longer they stayed, the more I learned what they needed, wanted and dreamed to have in their home. One very effective way was to put a stock pot on the stove. The fragrance of that broth worked like truth serum. The ingredients cost less than a dollar: a carrot, a medium onion, 2 ribs of celery, a bay leaf, and the carcass of this week's roasted chicken. Place all ingredients in a small stock pot and take to the site. As I turn on the lights, I cover the ingredients with water, and set on the range on low. At the end of the day, I take the finished chicken stock home and freeze it.

Butternut Squash Soup

Our son Drew made this soup on one of his visits from California. We were hosting our friends Scott and Penelope for dinner. Their daughters were also at the table. We were all concerned that the girls might not like this dish. Then we used Penelope's magic way of getting the girls to eat nearly anything. Just give the food an exotic name. Since Drew is a Rocket

Scientist, we called the soup "Spaceman's Squash Soup." It worked!

1 butternut squash (peeled) (5 pounds is a little too much)
Nutmeg
2 Tablespoons butter
salt
1 onion, chopped
6 Cups chicken stock

Cube butternut squash into 1 inch cubes. Sauté onions in butter until translucent. Add squash and stock. Cook until squash is tender, about 20-30 minutes. Puree squash chunks in food processor or blender until smooth. Return to pot. Season with salt, about 2 teaspoons if stock is unsalted--probably skip the salt entirely if using bouillon or stock with salt. Garnish with sour cream and nutmeg.

Cream of Pumpkin Soup

4 Tablespoons butter
1 large onion, thinly sliced
1 pumpkin, 4-5 pounds in weight
Nutmeg
Salt and pepper
1 Cup heavy cream

Wash and peel the pumpkin, remove the seeds and cut the flesh into cubes with a sharp knife. Set aside. Melt the butter in a large pot and add the onion. Sweat the onion slowly until it is fairly tender. Add the pumpkin chunks and 1 quart of cold water. Season with salt and pepper and a pinch of nutmeg. Simmer for 20 minutes. Puree the pumpkin mixture in small batches, adding cream to each small batch. Return the soup to the rinsed out pot and reheat gently. Serve hot.

Chicken and Sausage Gumbo

Gumbo is a soup with a hearty spicy nature and lots of body. When our son Drew was on the swim team in Louisiana, we would often make a huge kettle of the stuff starting with 6 stewing chickens. Then we would cook up at least ten pounds of rice to ladle the gumbo over, and sell it at swim meets as a fundraiser for the team. At $2.50 a bowl, it was a sell-out during the winter.

1 5 - 6 pound hen, cut into pieces
Salt, cayenne pepper, black pepper, Tabasco
Vegetable oil for browning, 1 to 1 ½ Cups
½ Cup flour
2 onions, diced
8 ribs of celery, chopped
1 large bell pepper, diced
1 teaspoon ground bay leaf
½ teaspoon thyme
1 teaspoon garlic powder
1 teaspoon celery seed
¼ teaspoon marjoram
1 gallon water
1 ½ pound sliced smoked sausage
1 Cup minced fresh parsley
1 pound okra, frozen is fine

Salt and pepper chicken, browning a large heavy pot in oil over medium heat. When well browned, remove chicken and set aside. Pour off all but ½ cup of the oil and add flour, browning well to make a dark roux. Reduce heat to low and add, onion, celery and green pepper. Sauté until soft, stirring regularly. Gradually add enough water to make a smooth sauce, stirring constantly. Add remaining water, chicken and other ingredients except the sausage, okra and parsley. Cook over medium heat for 1½ to 2 hours. Add sausage and okra in the last 45 minutes of cooking time. Remove and debone the chicken, discarding skin and bones. Return the chicken meat to the pot. Remove from heat, add the parsley and let stand for 15 minutes. Serve over rice.

Chili Macaroni

I must admit that I rather like the chili made in Texas. That spicy meat dish is absolutely nothing like the Chili I have served for many years. I make chili with beans served over macaroni with onions and cheese on top. It's spicier than most Midwestern versions but not near as hot as the Southwest versions. A certain chili cook-off at Langley Air Force Base comes to mind. One of Tony's co-workers on the staff from the RAF, "Wingco" made an entry for the contest with leftover roast beef and curry powder to bring up the heat. It was as unique a dish as anything we had ever eaten. Predictably, Bill didn't win the contest.

1 pound ground beef
1 onion
2 or 3 cloves garlic
2 teaspoons dry oregano leaves
3 Tablespoons chili powder
2 teaspoons ground cumin
2 One-pound cans chopped tomatoes
1 4-ounce can tomato paste
2 can dark red kidney beans
1 medium bell pepper chopped
2 Cups water
1 teaspoon salt
Black pepper
2 Cups elbow macaroni
Minced onion

Brown the ground beef and cook onion and garlic until translucent in a heavy large pan. Add seasoning, tomatoes and beans with juice. Bring to a boil and then simmer for about 1 hour. Adjust the seasoning. Cook the macaroni according to package instructions. If the chili is too thin, simmer to reduce the liquid. Add more water if it's too thick. Serve by placing cooked macaroni in the bottom of a soup bowl. Ladle the chili over the noodles. Top with fresh minced onion and a slice of American cheese.

Homemade Bean Soup

Vegetarians like this soup. Carnivorous families usually like some ham or smoked sausage added to the pot. It is quite tasty no matter how you put it together. When we were stationed at Yongsan Army Garrison in Korea, we shared a big pot of this soup with five or six friends. Along side a salad and crusty bread, the soup was washed down with several bottles of sparkling wine. It was at the end of the assignment and we were cleaning out the pantry. The wine was left from a promotion party and couldn't be shipped back to the States. One of those partaking remarked on how French the meal was. We were just frugal and not wanting to let the bubbly go to waste. After dinner it is suggested to light a few candles and open a couple windows. The gas can be pretty intense especially if you have sparkling wine too.

1 pound mixed beans
1 large onion
3 ribs celery
2 large cloves of garlic
2 14½-ounce cans whole tomatoes
1 Tablespoon olive oil
2 Bay leaves
1 Tablespoon dried basil
½ teaspoon Liquid Smoke
Salt and pepper to taste or a good dash of Creole seasoning
1 large carrot, diced

Takes a little time
Serves 6 to 8 as a main course
Serves 14 to 16 as a starter

Sort through the beans and discard any broken or unsightly beans. This is also a time to check for stones too. Rinse the beans and pour the water off through a strainer. Soak the beans in a large bowl with twice as much water as beans. Two Cups of beans should be covered with four Cups or even five or six of water. Soak overnight. Drain the beans and discard the water. Rinse again.

Chop the celery and onion. Crush the clove of garlic. Heat olive oil in large Dutch oven or heavy bottom soup pot. Sauté vegetables and garlic. Add beans, six Cups of water and the bay leaves and sweet basil. Bring to a boil. Reduce to a simmer and cooking 1 1/2 to 2 hours until the beans are tender. The longer you soaked the beans the less time they take to cook. All the beans should still have form with exception of the split peas. They should fall apart. The peas will be the last ones done. Crush or cut-up the tomatoes. Add the tomatoes, season with salt and pepper then simmer 15 more minutes. This is also a great time to add a few drops of liquid smoke. It gives a smoke taste with no meat and no fat. Taste the soup. Adjust the seasoning. If the soup is too thick or a few more people show-up, add water.

Serve the soup steaming hot in big bowls. Have a green salad and crusty bread on the side.

Marti's Italian Onion Soup

Whether you serve this as part of a big Italian dinner or with a sandwich for lunch, you'll find this lighter and less filling than the French version. The pasta boils up into tiny ball shapes. One of the gals at the Chosun Gift Shop in Korea went crazy for this soup, "Marti, when are you making the soup with the little balls in it?" Everyone in ear shot cracked up with laughter, but all knew which soup she meant. My broker in Atlanta, Nancy, thought that this soup was a very good use of Vidalia Onions and said something about it being one of the best soups she had eaten. It was a very nice compliment.

4 Cups thinly sliced onions
2 to 3 Tablespoons olive oil
5 Cups beef broth canned or 5 Cups water with bouillon cubes
1/3 cup ancini di pepe (very small peppercorn shaped pasta)
Italian firm aged cheese

Sautee onions in olive oil until translucent but not brown. Add beef broth and simmer for 45 min. Cook pasta in boiling water until tender. Drain. Add to soup. Serve hot in bowls with shredded Romano or Locatelli or Pecorino cheese for a garnish. I use a "V" slicer or mandolin to slice onions. Serves 8

135

Minestrone

If you haven't guessed from my last name, I am married to a person of Italian heritage. In the early years of our marriage, that meant having spaghetti every Sunday with the leftovers on Tuesday night. Some of Tony's favorites include spaghetti with sausage, peppers and onion; pork ribs simmered in spaghetti sauce; and of course chicken that has spent hours bubbling away in a rich red spaghetti sauce and served over angel hair pasta. I guess it goes back to his roots, when cooking over a campfire was a normal part of life, and cooking outdoors as an eagle scout was something he excelled at. In fact, we still use some recipes that were developed and fine tuned from his days as a ranger at Philmont Scout Camp.

I could give you a very long involved red sauce recipe, but I've found that jar sauce works just as well if seasoned to taste with extra basil and oregano. Just use your favorite sauce, cover the meat, add a few mushroom, peppers, and onions and cook it in a crock pot or on extremely low on top of the stove. When dark haired people of Mediterranean descent start hanging around the door mentioning that something smells great, cook up some pasta, grate some fresh Romano Cheese and enjoy. Our first soup is more like a "sweep the kitchen" vegetable soup, the second is more like a beefy stew.

Minestrone

¼ pound lean bacon, finely diced
2½ quarts water
1 16-ounce can whole tomatoes, undrained, chopped
1 15-ounce can red kidney beans, undrained
1 15-ounce can white kidney beans, undrained
6 beef flavor bouillon cubes
1 Cup diced carrot
1 Cup diced celery
1 Cup shredded cabbage
1 Cup green onion
1 10-ounce pkg. frozen chopped spinach

1 teaspoon. dried whole basil
½ teaspoon. freshly ground pepper
¾ Cup uncooked macaroni
Grated Parmesan cheese

Sauté bacon in a large Dutch oven until crisp; drain. Add remaining ingredients except for the macaroni and cheese. Bring to boil. Cover, reduce heat and simmer 1 hour. Add macaroni; simmer 10 minutes. Sprinkle each serving with cheese. Yield 18 Cups.

Minestra

The community pot was always on the fire in every home in Italy, and a lot of other countries too. Into it was started the meal for the day, which evolved into the meals for the week. Minestra (or Panagote) is simply "soup", and was comprised of whatever you had around, including a piece of meat, if you were lucky. It was soup on the first day, then maybe stew on the second, with the cook adding whatever it needed throughout the week. Sometimes cornmeal was added to thicken it into a mush, and would be eaten hot, with the leftovers being saved and baked the next day for an entirely different meal. These recipes use measurements by handfuls, or "about" this or that much. Taste it as you go and adjust as necessary.

For the Minestra, using a slow cooker, fill with a couple quarts of water, and add the meat, usually in 1-2 inch cubes. Cook on low until the meat is fork tender, or about 2 hours. Then season with 1-2 teaspoons beef bouillon, 3 Tablespoons parsley, 3 Tablespoons garlic powder, 3 Tablespoons Italian seasoning mix, 1 ½ teaspoons salt,. Add 3 potatoes, peeled and quartered into 2 inch cubes, and add your greens (escarole, endive or whatever). Cook on low for two more hours, and check seasoning, and serve.

Vegetarian Minestrone Stew

There are certain days in military life quite unlike civilian life. One of those is the day when a promotion list is made public. When we were in Korea the second time, Tony was eligible for promotion to colonel. The day the list was due to be published, I was a wreck. Usually someone would hint, whether those in the zone had made it or not, a couple of days in advance. For this promotion, there had been no advanced warning. I worked all day at the Chosun Gift shop. Of course I was useless that day -- I could only think about Tony. Had he made the list or not? I got home from work and decided after an hour or so that I had to do something. Cooking always quiets my nerves. I called my next-door neighbor and invited the two of them for dinner. I was feeling better. Finally, the phone rang. It was Tony calling from his hooch in Ouijongbu. He was on the list and was on his way home to celebrate.

This Vegetarian Minestrone Stew would be the meal for our party. Our friends Sam and Chuckie had dinner with us. As they left for home, Tony whispered to me, "Marti, I think you forgot to put the meat in the stew. There wasn't any in my bowl."

"Tony, vegetarian means no meat."

1 large onion, large dice
4 ribs celery, ½ inch pieces
2-3 large carrots, chunks
Olive oil
3 cloves garlic, minced
2 medium zucchini, 1-inch pieces
1 large green bell pepper, 1-inch pieces
8-ounces fresh mushrooms, quartered
2 teaspoons dried basil
2 bay leaves
1 teaspoon dried oregano
1 16-ounce can kidney beans
2 16-ounce cans diced tomatoes
1 quart tomato or V-8 juice

Salt, pepper, and pepper flakes (optional) to taste
½ pound macaroni or other medium sized pasta
Shredded Italian cheese

Sauté the onion, celery and carrots to soften in a small amount of olive oil. Then stir in garlic, zucchini, bell pepper, mushrooms, basil, bay leaves, and oregano. Sauté a few more minutes. Add the kidney beans including the juice from the can, the tomatoes and tomato juice. Season with salt, pepper and red pepper flakes. Simmer for at least 1 hour. Cook pasta to package directions, drain and rinse. Adjust the seasoning.

Serve in large soup bowls with pasta on the bottom of the bowl, the stew ladled on top and finished with a coat of shredded cheese.

Red wine and crusty bread are a must with this meal.

Polenta

Tony told his cousin Don, that he wanted to recreate Grandma's Polenta recipe, and when we went to visit over Christmas one year, Don thought he was joking. Thankfully he's a good cook in his own right, and helped Tony understand this wonderful staple.

Using a soup (about a quart of the Minestra) as a base, shred the meat into small bits, and cut up the greens. Bring to a boil, and then slowly **sprinkle** with cornmeal (about a cup), stirring constantly to avoid lumping. Add enough cornmeal and cook as you go over very low heat, until you get the desired consistency. Adding more corn meal will result in a thicker dish, but cooking will also thicken it too. Cook until it is no longer "grainy" to the taste. Serve hot, perhaps with a side of sauce, or let cool, and bake, cutting it into squares or strips.

Pea Soup with Hominy & Ham

Whole dried peas are my preference in this dish. Split peas don't have the same texture. In a time when we can get nearly anything in a supermarket, I have found that specialty stores are the only source for whole dried peas. Try a Korean market or a vegetarian foods store. When all else fails use split peas. The ham bones are easily found at the spiral baked ham stores. They also have a good amount of meat on them.

1 pound dried whole peas
1 ham bone
1 medium onion, diced
2 ribs of celery, diced
2 1-pound cans white or yellow hominy
Water
Salt and pepper

Soak the peas over night or at least 6 hours. Drain the water from the peas and rinse thoroughly. In a heavy soup pot add the peas, onion, celery and ham bone. Cover with water and at least 3 inches more water over the ingredients. Bring to a boil and then reduce to simmer. Cook for 2 to 2 ½ hours or until the peas are tender. More water maybe needed during the cooking process. When the peas are tender they will make the soup thick and the skins will hold their shape. Remove the ham and hambone from the soup. Cool. Dice meat and return to the soup pot. Drain the hominy and add to the soup. Simmer another 15 minutes. Adjust the seasoning with salt and pepper. If the soup is too thick, add more water. If it is too thin, reduce the volume by boiling. Serve soup hot with corn bread.

This soup will freeze well and will keep several months in the freezer.

Gazpacho Soup

This is one of those recipes that you really have to "add a pinch of this and a pinch of that". Vary the ingredients to your liking and put in more or less of whatever you like. The secret is to include a wide variety of what you like best, and vary the vegetables so that there is an interesting mix of consistencies. Then, when all the veggies are mixed, add enough liquid to make it a "soup" rather than a lumpy pile. I prefer V-8, then season and add a dash or few of hot sauce to spice it up! While we like this one cold and chunky, you can also run this mixture through the food processor to get it pureed. Stop short of making it completely smooth so as to give it some texture. Serve chilled on a hot summer's day.

4 Cups tomato juice, chilled (V-8 works if that is your taste)
2 cucumbers, peeled, seeded and finely diced
1 finely diced large bell pepper
4 to 6 large tomatoes diced
2 cloves garlic mashed through a garlic press
1 rib celery, minced
6 to 8 radishes, minced
2 Tablespoons olive oil
2 or 3 Tablespoons red wine vinegar
¼ Cup parsley, minced
Pepper
Salt
2 Tablespoons fresh basil, finely chopped
1 scallion, finely chopped
1 Tablespoon Worcestershire
1 Tablespoon lemon juice
Dash Tabasco

Combine all. Serve with a dollop of sour cream and some snipped chives. Serves 4.

Potato Leek Soup

My French grandmother could make soup out of most anything. There was the chicken soup, clam chowder; beef with tomatoes and rice, and of course the potato soup. On Fridays when we ate no meat this soup started dinner. The following course was the fried fish. Usually the fish werethe ones caught during the summer fishing trip. The Walleyed Pike was and still is one of my favorites. Of course filets of fish did not exist. The fish had been gutted and scaled. The heads were also left behind. The bones were something we learned to bypass. If you couldn't deal with the bones, you ate more soup.

2 to 2½ pounds baking potatoes
1 Large leek
1 medium onion
2 Cups chicken broth
Water
1 egg
1 Cup all purpose flour
2 large cans evaporated milk
2 Tablespoons of butter
¼ Cup minced parsley
Salt and pepper to taste

Peel and cut the potatoes into ½ inch slices. Set aside in a bowl of cold water to cover. Carefully clean the leek. There is sand "hiding" between the leaves. Slice the leeks into thin crosscut strips. Use the green and the white. Dice the onion. Place all these ingredients in a soup pot. Add the chicken stock and enough water to cover the vegetables plus 2 to 3 additional inches of liquid. Bring to a boil, reduce and simmer until tender.

Meanwhile, place a cup of flour in a deep small bowl that is about a 2 cup size or so. Make a well in the center of the flour. Break the egg into the flour. With a fork beat the egg with a ½ teaspoon of salt until light in color without adding much of the flour from the sides. Gently begin to incorporate the flour until the egg and flour mixture is too thick for fork to work the dough.

Remove the fork and continue to work in more flour until a very stiff dough is created. Bring the soup back to a boil. Pinch off very small piece of the dough to create small dry dumplings in the soup. Add the parsley. Cook until the dumplings are tender.

Add the milk, adjust the seasoning, and never let the soup come to a boil again. The soup will curdle if boiled again, guaranteed at 100%! Finish with butter until melted and serve immediately. This soup will serve at least 8 people.

__Pumpkin Soup__
With Black Bean Salsa

When there's a chill in the air and the oaks and maple have changed colors, this soup takes the edge off the coolest of evenings.

1 Pie Pumpkin, peeled and cleaned
1 med Onion, diced
2 ribs celery, diced
1-2 teaspoons minced garlic
1 Box (1 quart) Swanson Chicken Broth
½ Cup butter
½ Cup flour
2 10-ounce cans evaporated milk
¾ teaspoon nutmeg
2 teaspoons Creole seasoning
Dehydrated potato flakes

Sauté onion & celery until translucent. Add garlic, cook 1 minute more. Cut pumpkin into 1-inch pieces. Pour in broth and add pumpkin. Bring to boil, reduce & cook until tender. Make a roux of butter & flour – set aside. Blend pumpkin stew with immersion blender until smooth. Or use a blender in small batches, never more than ½ the volume of the blender, to smooth the soup. Bring back to boil & whisk in all of the roux. Boil for at least one minute. Quickly add milk and cook to near boil. If too thick add water. If too thin add instant potato flakes. Season with a pinch of nutmeg & Creole seasoning.

Black Bean Salsa

1 can black beans, drained & rinsed
1 shallot, finely minced
Juice ½ lemon
½ medium red pepper ¼ inch dice
1 teaspoon white wine Worcestershire sauce
2 teaspoons hot sauce or any spicy steak sauce

Mix together and let rest. Spoon hot soup into cups. Garnish with a teaspoon or two of salsa. Serve at once.

Shrimp & Cheese Soup

This soup was created in the kitchen in our quarters at Yongsan Army Garrison in Korea. My friend Pam and I had dinner together and this soup was made from pantry items. Pam loved it and makes it as soon as the weather turns a bit on the cool side each year.

1 carrot, diced
1 stalk celery, diced
½ Cup onion, diced
1 Tablespoon vegetable oil
2 Cup chicken broth
½ teaspoon thyme
½ teaspoon marjoram
1/8 teaspoon Creole seasoning
4 Tablespoons melted butter
4 Tablespoons flour
1 Cup cooked salad shrimp
¾ Cup Velveeta
1 10-ounce can evaporated milk
1 Cup white wine

Dice all vegetables in 1/8-inch dice. It's a little trouble but makes a lovely presentation in the end. Sauté vegetables for 3 or 4 minutes in oil. Add broth and seasoning. Simmer for 5 minutes. Make a blonde roux with the butter and flour. Stir into the broth. Bring to a boil and simmer at least 1 to 2 minutes. Add the shrimp, cheese, evaporated milk and white wine. Simmer for 5 to 10 more minutes and serve.

<u>Turkey Soup/Stew</u>

2 ribs celery
2 leeks
½ yellow onion
2 Tablespoons oil
3 Cups chicken broth
½ teaspoon thyme
1 Tablespoon dried parsley
1½ Cups frozen mixed vegetables
2 potatoes
3 Cups leftover turkey

Chop the celery, slice the leeks, and chop the onion. Sauté the vegetables in oil until translucent in a Dutch oven or large heavy sauce pan. Add broth and herbs. Simmer for 15 minutes. Add the vegetables and 2 potatoes peeled and cut into chunks. Cut turkey into large chunks and add to the pot. Simmer until potatoes are fork tender. Make a blonde roux to thicken the broth. If soup is preferred over stew, skip the thickening.

Serve over biscuits or bake with a piecrust top. Dip into soup bowls or make dumplings in the brothy soup.

IX. Pasta and Bread

We sought out our second tour to Korea with two separate goals in mind. Tony was after another command position so he could compete better for promotion, and I wanted to get some international wholesale and retail buying experience by working with the Chosun Gift Shop, the largest American charity in the Pacific. We were successful in getting both.

Tony's job landed him within 5 miles of the Korean Demilitarized Zone, actually within mortar distance of the front line of troops. It was an eerie feeling, standing so close to the most heavily defended border in the entire world. And we would play war games on a daily basis, out of necessity. His quarters were a "hooch" at Camp Red Cloud just outside of Ouijongbu, and I had a small house at Yongsan Army Garrison in Seoul. I worked at the Chosun Gift Shop first as the stockroom manager, then the next year as the overall CEO and store manager. I was also the primary overseas buyer for this four million dollar a year business, going on buying trips as required to the Philippines, Thailand, Hong Kong, and Japan. Hong Kong was my favorite, and we even went there together once for a little R&R.

After Tony pinned on eagles, promoting him to colonel at a ceremony at the gift shop, we threw a party at our house with a chicken BBQ, and really had a houseful. Marinated chicken breasts on the outdoor barbeque, cooked slowly, turned out to be a very versatile dish. The secret is to marinate the breasts in a mix of 3 parts low fat to 1 part very spicy Italian salad dressing for several days, not just a couple hours. The marinade soaks deeply into the breasts and the vinegar does a little pre cooking. So as they slowly cook on the grill, the flavor is embedded deeply in the breast, and the meat stays moist. The same breast, when chilled then sliced, is simply outstanding when added to lettuce for Chicken Caesar Salad, or when added to your favorite pasta salad with sliced olives, cheeses and seasoned croutons, with a drizzle of Italian dressing over the top. Serve with fresh baked bread on the side.

Pumpkin Bread

I can't stand to see food go to waste. That includes pumpkins on Halloween. The small pumpkins are great to peel, clean of seeds and steam. The pumpkin is then run through a food mill. Freeze two- cup bags of pumpkin for soups and pumpkin bread.

3 Cups flour
1 teaspoons baking soda
1 teaspoon salt
3 teaspoons cinnamon
2 Cups cooked, mashed pumpkin
4 eggs, beaten
1¼ Cups vegetable oil
1 Cup chopped pecans

Add 2 Cups Sugar
To the Eggs and Oil !

    Preheat oven to 325 degrees.
    Sift dry ingredients together in a large bowl. Stir pumpkin, eggs and oil together. Make a well in the dry ingredients, add pumpkin mixture, and stir until smooth. Add nuts. Pour into 2 greased bread pans and bake for 45 minutes or until pick comes out clean.

Fresh Flour Tortillas

Making homemade tortillas is fun and the flavor beats the packaged versions. Make these to serve with the Mexican breakfasts for a brunch. Homemade tortillas are much more filling than store bought, so two tortillas per person will be plenty.

4 Cups all purpose flour
2 teaspoons salt
½ Cup shortening
1 Cup lukewarm water

Sift flour & salt into a mixing bowl. Add shortening, cut into the flour until well distributed. Add lukewarm water and blend well. Turn out on a lightly floured board and knead about 50 strokes. Divide dough into 12 equal pieces and form each piece into a ball. Cover with a damp cloth and let stand for 15 minutes. Roll each ball into an 8 inch diameter circle. Cook on a moderately hot ungreased skillet until golden brown in spots, turning once and being careful not to break air bubbles. Makes 12 tortillas.

Ravioli

1 8-ounce container ricotta cheese
4 ounces mozzarella cheese, shredded
½ Cup Parmesan cheese, grated
1 egg
½ Tablespoon parsley, chopped
Pinch of nutmeg   salt & pepper to taste

Ravioli dough is different than spaghetti dough. Use only eggs and flour, and once your dough ball is smooth and elastic, refrigerate for 1 hour to allow the flour to absorb the liquid. Then roll into a flat sheet. If using a pasta machine, don't use the thinnest setting, use the one just before. Place a dollop of filling near the end of the sheet, seal the edges with an egg wash (1 egg + 1 tsp water), then fold the top over, seal, then cut off. Make sure all the air is out of the pocket by pressing the edges. These are the large raviolis, and two or three is a meal. Freeze immediately for 3 hours. To cook, drop into boiling water, face down. When they float to the top, they're finished.

Fresh Sauce/Spaghetti

This takes about 35 minutes from start to finish. Serve over pasta with good fresh grating cheese, red wine and a salad. It's healthy and filling. Vary this recipe with the addition of one can drained and rinsed kidney beans. You may also grill or pan-fry Italian Sausage and then proceed with following instructions.

1 medium onion
2-3 ribs celery
1 large bell pepper
8 ounces fresh mushrooms
2 Tablespoons olive oil
¼ Cup fresh basil leaves
2-4 cloves fresh garlic
2 bay leaves
1 teaspoon dried marjoram
½ teaspoon dried thyme
Salt and pepper
2 cans of diced tomatoes

Cut onions, celery, and bell pepper into 1- inch pieces. Cut mushrooms into quarters. Sauté in olive oil for a couple of minutes. Season with basil, cloves garlic, bay leaves, marjoram, thyme, salt and fresh ground black pepper. Add 2 cans diced tomatoes. Simmer 30 minutes. Serve over pasta.

Italian Bread

2 Cups water
2 packages dry yeast
1 Tablespoon sugar
1 Tablespoon salt
5½ - 6 ½ Cups bread flour
Oil
Cornmeal

In hot water, approximately 120 degrees, dissolve salt sugar and yeast. Beat in 2 Cups of the flour with an electric mixer until the gluten forms. It will look stringy and somewhat snotty. Change to the bread hooks and stir in the balance of the flour until the ball forms. Remove from mixer and knead. Use 1 teaspoon of oil, oil a bowl and the dough, cover with wet tea towel or plastic wrap, set in a warm place and let double in bulk.

Punch down, divide into two portions, and knead each of the portions 15 strokes. Place in 2 oiled bowls, cover and let rise.

Punch down the dough and roll on lightly floured surface to a rectangle about 9 x 12. Roll long side in toward center, pushing out the air as you go and pinching it. Pinch the seam firmly, karate chop the ends and turn them under. Place the loaf on a cookie sheet sprinkled with corn meal, seam side down, lightly oil the top, cover with plastic wrap, let rise until double in bulk. If you gently poke your finger into the side of the loaf, and the dent stays, it's ready. Shape both loaves.

Take 1 egg white with a teaspoon of water, and beat until lightly frothy. Brush each loaf with egg white mixture, sprinkle with sesame or poppy seeds, cut 3-4 diagonal gashed, ½ inch deep in each loaf, and bake at 375 degrees until golden brown, and the loaf sounds hollow when tapped.

Holiday Banana Bread

My mother, Mary Lorraine Emling, worked for several years at a pharmaceutical plant labeling medications. While there she picked up a couple of good recipes from friends. This is one of those recipes that my sisters and I liked and my sons just expected. Nick says the best part of banana bread is the cherries. This recipe also makes great muffins. Bake at the same temperature and remove when the tops are nicely browned and a toothpick inserted comes out clean.

1 egg
1 Cup sugar
½ Cup margarine
3 bananas
1 teaspoon vanilla
2 Cups flour
1 teaspoon baking soda
1 Cup Maraschino cherries
½ Cup pecans or walnuts chopped

Preheat oven to 350 degrees. With and electric mixer beat sugar and margarine until fluffy. Add eggs. Mash bananas and mix in thoroughly. Stir in vanilla. Sift flour and baking soda together. Mix in flour slowly until a light batter is formed. Drain and chop cherries. Stir in cherries and nuts. Pour into an oiled 9 x 5 x 3 pan. Bake in preheated oven for 1 hour and 15 minutes.

Pizza Dough

One year Tony and the boys selected the menu for Christmas. This was not my wisest move. We had a more formal dinner on Christmas Eve and then on Christmas Day we ate pizza for dinner. For me, it just wasn't the right meal for Christmas Day. We changed the order of the meals the next year and now our family tradition is to make pizza for Christmas Eve dinner. Whether you choose to go all the way with homemade sausage, homemade sauce, and a variety of meats, cheeses and vegetables is up to you. If you use sausage or ground beef, brown the meat before topping the pizza. Sauté bell peppers, onions, and fresh mushrooms to tenderize.

Here are a couple of fun ideas for homemade pizzas: Make 2 large pizza crusts in jelly roll pans. After the pre-cooking of the bread, cool one on a wire rack, store in a plastic bag in the freezer for up to a month for another "fresh" pizza later. Or, make lots of smaller crusts. Bake until firm. Cool and place between layers of wax paper. Arrange a buffet of all kinds of topping and let your guests make their own personal size pizza. The small pies bake quickly. It's also fun for the guests or family and makes an event of dinner. At one party we had one guest eat only cheese, no sauce. Another guest had no cheese, no meat and ate sauce with vegetables. Of course there were the pepperoni folks and those who put everything not nailed down on their "personal pies."

2 Cups very warm water
2 packages yeast
2 Cups flour (to start)
1 Tablespoon sugar
1 Tablespoon salt
3½ to 4 Cups flour and oil as needed for shaping

Beat with mixer until stringy, stir in enough flour to make dough stiff (5 ½ to 6 Cups total). Let rise in a warm area to double in bulk. Punch down and knead 12 strokes, divide in half, let rise again until double. Punch down and shape. Moisten top with oil, and let rise a bit while oven warms. Cook crust in oven at 425 for about 10 minutes or until the edges just start to brown.

Remove from oven, place toppings on, and slide back into oven for another 30 minutes, or until the cheese melts and begins to bubble. Remove before cheese browns/burns.

Cut pizza with scissors. Use long handle scissors to avoid hot knuckles. Slip the pie on a cutting board and clip away.

Noodles For Soup

*Use this same recipe for making spaghetti noodles. You can also use a pasta machine to flatten the dough before you roll it up to cut it, or if you have the attachments, to run it though the slicing blades. You can add a lot of character to these homemade noodles by adding some basil or thyme to the dough while it is still very moist. Once it gets to the doughy stage, it's a little harder to work with. Try other seasonings that are green for flavor, like parsley or chopped spinach that you've squeezed **all** the moisture out of, or other greens.*

2 Cups of flour
2 eggs
½ teaspoon salt

Make a well in the flour. Break eggs into the well. Whip with a fork while slowly incorporating flour from side of the well. Continue until mixture is too thick to use fork. Knead with fingers in the bowl adding additional flour until noodle dough is hard and fairly smooth.

Divide into two balls and rollout until paper-thin. Keep flouring as you go so it won't stick. Flour again after thin enough and roll up like a jellyroll.

Cut into strips. Toss to unwind. Cook in boiling broth.

Lasagna

1 pound Italian sausage
1 clove garlic, minced
1 Tablespoon basil, dried
1½ teaspoons salt
1 1-pound can whole tomatoes, chopped, undrained
2 6-ounce cans tomato paste
10 ounces lasagna noodles
2 eggs
3 Cups fresh Ricotta or cream style cottage cheese
½ Cup grated Parmesan or Romano cheese
2 Tablespoons parsley flakes, dried
1 teaspoon pepper
1 pound Mozzarella cheese, sliced very thin

Brown meat slowly; spoon off excess fat. Add next 5 ingredients and 1 cup water. Simmer, covered, 15 minutes; stir often. Cook noodles according to package directions in boiling water. Beat eggs; add remaining ingredients except for mozzarella.

Layer half the noodles in a 13x9x2 inch baking dish; spread with half the Ricotta fillings; add half the mozzarella cheese and half the meat sauce. Repeat. Bake at 375 degrees about 30 minutes. If you assemble this early and refrigerate increase baking time to 45 minutes. Let stand 10 minutes before serving. Serves 8 to 10.

Spinach Lasagna

Delete the sausage in the recipe above. Defrost one pound frozen chopped spinach. Squeeze the moisture from the spinach. Add the spinach to the egg-ricotta mixture and proceed as above.

White Bread

This is the real deal. Either share the loaves with a neighbor or freeze the extras. Always use a bread knife to slice.

2 Cups milk
¾ Cup sugar
8 teaspoons salt
¾ Cup margarine
6 Cups warm water
4 packages dry yeast
24 Cups all purpose flour (about)

Scald milk; stir in sugar, salt and margarine. Cool to lukewarm. Pour warm water into a very large bowl. Sprinkle in yeast; stir until dissolved. Add milk mixture and about half the flour. Use a mixer to beat until smooth. Add enough additional flour to make a stiff dough. Turn out onto a lightly floured board; knead until smooth and elastic, about 10 to 12 minutes. Place in greased bowl, turning to grease top. Cover and let rise in warm place, free from draft, until doubled in bulk, about 1 hour.

Punch dough down. Cover; let rest 15 minutes. Divide dough into 6 equal pieces. Roll each piece to a 14 x 9-inch rectangle. Shape into loaves. Place in 6 greased loaf pans.

Whole Wheat Bread

Baking bread and making soup have to be on the top of my favorite cooking lists. There's something so complete about a crusty loaf with a big ladle of soup. For the three months we lived in Tucson while Tony was training in the A-10, I decided to make all our bread. Of course Tony and I thought this was a very good thing to do. Our sons, Nick and Drew, were not as impressed. They pooled allowance money at one point and bought a loaf of "real" bread from a store. Yes, it was the white "spongy stuff."

2 Cups milk
½ Cup light brown sugar, firmly packed
1 teaspoon salt
¼ Cup butter or regular margarine
1 Cup warm water (105-115 degrees)
2 packages active dry yeast
8 Cups unsifted whole-wheat flour
Additional all purpose flour
Butter for the top of the loaf

In a saucepan heat milk until bubbles form around the edge. Remove from heat. Add sugar, salt, ¼ cup butter. Stir until the butter melts. Cool. Sprinkle yeast over water in a large mixing bowl. Stir to dissolve the yeast. Then add the milk mixture. If using a big kitchen mixer use the regular paddle and beat until smooth. If your doing this with a wooden spoon, make sure you've kept-up working your upper body at the gym. If using the mixer, change to the dough hook. Gradually add the rest of the flour and knead by machine until it comes away from the sides of the bowl and is smooth looking. If using the hand method, stir the rest of the flour gradually. The dough will be very stiff. Turn out on a floured board and knead by hand for 8 to 10 minutes. Use regular all-purpose flour on the board. Oil a very large bowl. Place the ball of dough in the bowl. Roll it around to coat the dough with oil. Cover with plastic wrap and let rise until double in the warm draft free place. This will take about an hour. Punch down the dough. Turn out on the lightly floured board. Halve the dough and shape into loaves. Place in well-greased bread pans. Oil the tops of the loaves. Cover with plastic wrap and let rise a second time. Bake in a preheated 400 degree oven for 35 to 40 minutes. Remove bread from pans as soon as possible after baking. Let cool on racks. To slice, turn on the side. Use a sawing motion and a serrated knife.

Yorkshire Pudding

The first time I ate this dish, I was about 9 years old. We had a neighbor from Canada who always made Yorkshire pudding when she roasted beef. When you grow up in the mid-west, mashed or boiled potatoes are nearly always served with a roast. This was quite an unusual item for our family back then. Of course after marriage, unusual for my family was reserved for those foods that couldn't be described without a lesson in geography.

1 Cup cold milk
1 Cup all purpose flour
2 eggs
½ teaspoon salt.

Beat all ingredients with a whisk or hand mixer until smooth. Pour into a well-oiled Pyrex pie pan. When the roast is finished remove from oven and let rest for 20 to 25 minutes. Turn the heat up to 425 degrees. Slide the Yorkshire pudding into the oven. Bake for 25 minutes or longer. The steam in the batter makes this dish rise. When it is brown and bumpy like mountains it's done. Take immediately to the table. As it cools it will deflate like a balloon. Cut in wedges and serve with beef gravy.

X. Desserts

The final chapter to any great meal is the dessert that the chef prepares, and it is the last thing that remains in the mouth and stays on the mind of the guests. So it was with the final chapter of the "Road Show", Tony's assignment to Atlanta, Georgia in 1998 as the Air Force advisor to Lt Gen Tommy Franks, the Third Army commander. We arrived at a rather tense time in the Persian Gulf, with Saddam Hussein kicking up his heels at the world. Our command and control function as the Army component headquarters was needed in Kuwait three times in the first six months after we got here, so traveling east became a habit. Later, Tony's retirement ceremony was held on the very same parade field at Fort McPherson where his mother and father had first met, back in 1944, while learning how to march.

Every culture we've encountered has dessert. Some are more to our liking than others. There is mango pudding in Hong Kong, delicate pastries from Europe are paired with aged cheeses and fruit, and of course there is ice cream. In Kansas, the Kansas State University Dairy Lab sold very rich ice creams supported by 19% butterfat. In Kuwait, the dining hall contractor got a bonus if the ice cream was better than in the states, and he got bonuses all the time! And every meal with his ice cream was an upper for the GI's – the wait at the ice cream line was usually longer than the line at the door. No matter what the locale, we have tried them all. That "something sweet" at the end of the meal or as a middle-of-

the-afternoon boost can be simple or complicated. The easiest desserts of fruit with a little syrup are often the most healthy too.

Bread Pudding with Whiskey Sauce

3 Cups milk
2 Tablespoons butter
3 eggs
½ Cup sugar
½ teaspoon salt

Grease a 9x12 baking dish and fill with 1 inch cubes of day old bread. Sprinkle with raisins. Scald the milk and butter. Beat the eggs, sugar and salt together. Slowly add the scalded milk. Pour over bread. Place the 9x12 dish in a larger pan filled with water. Bake at 350 degrees for 45 minutes.

The sauce:
¼ pound butter
¾ Cup sugar
3 Tablespoons milk
4 Tablespoons whiskey

Cream the butter and sugar. Add milk and whiskey and mix together. Heat over low heat. Cut the pudding in squares. Put in a bowl or on a plate. Ladle sauce on top.

Bourbon Balls

During our second tour in Korea, I had a day that was quite a bit of fun. The guys and gals that were under Tony's command got to make cookies for a day during December. I made up batches of sugar cookie dough and brought supplies to make tons of other flavors. We made all sorts of confections including these classics. We sent grocery sacks of cookies to an orphanage but kept the Bourbon Balls and a few dozen other cookies for the

Brandied Peach Dessert pg 162

Cookies pg 166

Pineapple Upsidedown Cake pg 176

Toffee pg 184

party in the recreation room that evening. One of the younger airmen ate 12 of these and got a bit high. Yes, they are potent. On that one day in Korea, the ASOCS (Air Support Operations Center Squadron) smelled like a kitchen in the States even though we were mere miles from the DMZ (Korean Demilitarized Zone). That was fun.

1 pound vanilla wafers, crushed
2 Cups nuts, chopped
2 Tablespoons cocoa
2 Cups powdered sugar
3 Tablespoons light corn syrup
4 ounces Bourbon or rum
Extra powdered sugar

Place all dry ingredients in large bowl. Mix thoroughly. Make a well in the middle of the dried mixture. Set the mixture aside. In a small bowl mix syrup and liquor. Pour into the well. Incorporate the liquid into the dry. Form balls. Then roll in powdered sugar. Store in an airtight container until ready to eat/serve.

<u>Crusty Cherry/Berry Pie</u>

My sister Michele gets thanks for this fruit pie that has a nice crunchy crust. And it's very easy, allowing you to look wonderful in the kitchen without much effort.

1 Can pie filling (your favorite fruit)
½ Cup chopped nuts (pecans)
½ Cup dried oatmeal (quick or regular oats)
3 Tablespoons brown sugar
3 Tablespoons melted butter

Mix thoroughly and spread over your filled pie crust. Bake as normal, following cooking directions on the can of pie filling

Brandied Peach Dessert

I think that this was our son Drew's favorite dessert. It has a nice presentation and a subtle combination of flavors. The difference in textures is also interesting. If you haven't canned your own brandied peaches, just pour 1/3 cup of inexpensive brandy into canned peaches and set aside in the refrigerator for a week or so. If there are any left at the end of a week, make the dessert. Do not pour the syrup down the sink. Pour it over pound cake or ice cream. All right, you can sip on it like a cordial too.

4 Brandied peach halves
2 Cups homemade vanilla pudding (Blanc Mange)
1 Cup fresh or frozen whole raspberries

In a stemmed glass like an American Champagne glass, place ½ cup of the pudding. Top with a peach half, the round portion facing up. Surround with the berries. Cover with plastic wrap and refrigerate a couple of hours.

Brandied Peaches

These are definitely not canned peaches for the children. They make a lovely dessert with ice cream or with pudding. Serve alone with the accompanying syrup for a simple ending to a meal. Brandied peaches are a labor of love. It's far easier to buy peaches in jar or can and add some brandy to them. If you don't mind canning when the peaches are ready, and taking at least one whole afternoon to do it, then go ahead. This is nasty staining work. Anything a peach touches will turn it brown. Working over pots of boiling water or syrup in the dead of summer is also not fun. Then of course you need to wait at least 4 to 6 weeks before opening them for the first time. But when the time comes to open the peaches it's really special. Here are jewels for the bowl. You did it.

Peaches
Fruit Fresh
Simple Syrup
Brandy

Select firm and ripe peaches that have a pleasing color. Pale peaches will not have as much flavor as those with "rosy" cheeks. Slip the skins from the peaches by immersing in a pot for boiling water for 30 seconds and then into iced water that has been treated with Fruit Fresh to ward off discoloring and browning.

Prepare heavy syrup of 1 cup of water to 1 cup sugar for each pound of peaches. Simmer the peaches for 5 minutes in the syrup. Remove with a slotted spoon and arrange the peaches, cut side down, in canning jars. Add 2 Tablespoons of brandy for each pint or ¼ cup brandy for a quart jar. Fill the jars with the simmered syrup by pouring the syrup over the fruit and removing any air bubbles. Seal and process the jars in a water bath for 15 minutes. Store in a cool dark place. Use inexpensive brandy for this dish. Save the sipping stuff for friends who can appreciate it. There is too much sugar in the peaches to use the good stuff.

Pralines

1½ Cup white sugar
¾ Cup firmly packed brown sugar
¼ Cup plus 2 Tablespoons butter
½ Cup milk
1½ Cup chopped pecans

Lightly coat wax paper with vegetable oil spray and set aside. Combine sugar, brown sugar, and remaining ingredients in a heavy 3 quart saucepan. Bring to a boil over medium heat, stirring constantly. Boil uncovered, stirring constantly until candy thermometer reaches 220 degrees. Remove from heat and beat with wooden spoon 4-6 minutes or until mixture begins to thicken. Working rapidly, drop by tablespoonfuls onto wax paper. Let stand until firm.

Drew's Almond Cheese Cake

This cheesecake is just sweet enough to satisfy and perfect for eight servings in size. There is no substitute for the spring form pan. Be sure to check which is the correct way to put the pan together to prevent a messy disaster.

1 Cup vanilla wafer crumbs
¼ Cup melted butter
¼ Cup sugar
¼ Cup almond slices
16 ounces cream cheese at room temperature
4 eggs
1 Cup sugar
Pinch of salt
1 teaspoon almond extract
1 Cup sour cream
¼ Cup sugar
¼ teaspoon almond extract

Beat cream cheese with mixer until fluffy. Add eggs, 1 at a time, beating constantly. When thoroughly mixed, blend 1 cup sugar, salt and almond extract in slowly.

Mix together wafer crumbs, butter, ¼ cup sugar and almond slices. Press into 9 inch spring form pan. Pour in cheesecake mixture. Bake for 45 minutes at 350 degrees in a pre-heated oven.

Pull open door and pull cake out on rack. Spread sour cream mixture on cake and return to oven for 15 minutes. Remove from oven and cool thoroughly followed by 3 to 4 hours or over night refrigeration.

Chocolate Fudge Sour Cream Cake

My friend Sandy told us at a real estate agent training session, that when you have a luncheon for an agent open house or any real estate event, there must be chocolate. I have found that this cake fits that order as well as many a birthday party or other celebration. The chocolate kisses aren't necessary but they do make the cake look rather festive. You can also coat the sides of the cake with chocolate sprinkles if you want to really go over the top and then apply the kisses.

¼ Cup margarine
2 Cups sugar
¾ Cup sour cream
4 ounces unsweetened chocolate, melted and then cooled
2 eggs
1¼ teaspoons baking soda
1 teaspoon salt
½ teaspoon baking powder
1 teaspoon vanilla
2 Cups flour
1 Cup water

With an electric mixer in a large bowl, cream together the margarine, sugar, sour cream and eggs. Stir in the chocolate. Add the baking soda, salt, baking powder and vanilla. Stir together. Then add the flour and water adding half of each at a time and mixing until incorporated. Beat at high speed for 3 minutes if using a stand mixer or 4 minutes if using an electric hand mixer. Scrape the sides of the bowl occasionally. For a taller cake use oiled 8 inch layer pans and bake 35 to 40 minutes at 350 degrees until a cake tester is inserted and comes out clean. For a very portable cake use a 9x13 inch pan and bake 40 to 45 minutes. Frost with Chocolate Sour Cream Frosting below.

Chocolate Sour Cream Frosting

½ Cup butter or margarine
2 ounces unsweetened chocolate, melted and then cooled
1/3 Cup sour cream
2½-3 Cups powdered sugar
2 teaspoons vanilla
Chocolate kisses and sprinkles as desired

With an electric mixer stir together the chocolate, butter and sour cream. Beat in the powdered sugar. Add slowly or plan to clean the kitchen thoroughly after making this frosting. Stir in the vanilla. Beat until light and smooth. Spread on the top of the bottom layer a couple dollops of the frosting for a filling. Then frost the top and sides. Decorate as desired.

Triple Chocolate Cookies

1 Cup sugar
½ Cup softened margarine
1 egg
2 ounces melted unsweetened chocolate
1/3 Cup buttermilk
1 teaspoon vanilla
1¾ Cups all purpose flour
½ teaspoon baking soda
½ teaspoon salt
1 Cup miniature semi-sweet chocolate chips
1 Cup chopped nuts
Chocolate frosting

Preheat oven to 400 degrees. Mix sugar, margarine, egg, chocolate, buttermilk and vanilla. Stir in flour, baking soda, salt, nuts, and mini chips. Drop dough by rounded teaspoons about 2 inches apart onto ungreased cookie sheet. Bake until almost no indentation remains when touched, 8 to 10 minutes. Immediately remove from cookie sheet and cool on a rack. Frost with Chocolate Frosting.

Chocolate Frosting

2 squares of unsweetened chocolate
2 Tablespoons margarine
3 Tablespoons water
2 Cups powdered sugar

Heat chocolate and margarine over low hear or in microwave until melted. Beat in water and then powder sugar. The powdered sugar is an approximate measurement and may take a little more or a little less. Beat until smooth and spreads easily.

Carrot Cake

Maybe we should just call this Tony's birthday, promotion, and retirement cake. Every time an event came up, this cake with cream cheese frosting was Tony's choice. It's easy to make, tastes good, and you can put a variety of frostings on it, and it makes a good base for cutting up for different theme shapes. Ensure it's cooked completely by using the toothpick test.

2 Cups sugar
3 Cups all purpose flour
1 teaspoon baking soda
2 teaspoons cinnamon
½ teaspoon salt
1½ Cups vegetable oil
1 teaspoon lemon extract
1 Cup undrained crashed pineapple
2 Cups grated carrots
1 Cup chopped pecans
1 Cup dried currants
1½ teaspoons lemon peel.

Preheat oven to 350 degrees. Sift dry ingredients together. Add remaining ingredients in order, blending well. I use a wooden spoon in a big bowl for this cake. Bake in a greased 9x13 inch pan for 35-45 minutes.

167

Cowboy Cookies

I began making these cookies when Tony and I were first married. As a cook for a sorority house at the University of Illinois, I made 4 times the batch every Monday morning. When our son Drew was swimming, I made the cookies in a jelly roll pan and cut them into bars, and presto, swimmer's bars. Put fruitcake fruit into the batter instead of chocolate chips and you have Christmas cookies. Be sure to work with these quickly out of the oven when you're doing the Christmas version, they have more sugar in them and they set-up fast. When I offered my grandson his first Cowboy Cookie he said, "I'm not sure about this." Our son Nick was crushed! How could his son not love the same cookies he had grown up with! Have a good time with the recipe. Vary the dried fruits to your taste.

2 Cups flour
½ teaspoon salt
1 teaspoon soda
½ teaspoon baking powder
1 Cup margarine
1 Cup sugar
1 Cup brown sugar, firmly packed
2 eggs
1 teaspoon vanilla
2 Cups quick oats
1 Cup nuts (walnuts, pecans or hazelnuts)
1 6-ounce package chocolate chips
1 Cup raisins

Mix together the first 4 ingredients in a bowl. Set aside. In the mixer, cream together the sugar and margarine. Add the eggs one at a time. Mix each thoroughly. Beat until light and fluffy. Mix in the vanilla. Carefully stir in the flour ½ Cup at a time. Then stir in the oats. Follow with the chocolate chips, nuts and raisins. Drop by teaspoonfuls onto a greased or vegetable sprayed coated pan. Bake at 350 degrees for about 15 minutes. Cool on racks. Makes 8 to 10 dozen. Store in an airtight container.

Delicate Lemon Bars

Believe it or not there are a few times that a chocolate dessert is just not the right thing. That's when you should serve a nice plate of lemon squares. These bars are just sweet enough with the perfect amount of tang. They also make a lovely balance for a buffet dessert when the other selections are rich chocolate delights. Unfortunately these will not hold overnight.

¼ pound butter
1 Cup sifted flour
¼ Cup confectioner's sugar
2 Tablespoons flour
½ teaspoon baking powder
2 eggs
1 Cup sugar
3 Tablespoons lemon juice

Mix first 3 ingredients together with a pastry blender. Press evenly into 9x9x2 inch pan (moisten fingers to avoid sticking). Bake for 15 minutes at 350.

Mix remaining ingredients and pour over baked bottom layer. Return to oven for 20-25 minutes. Do not overcook. Top should be a little soft. Cut into fingers or squares when cool and sprinkle with additional confectioners sugar.

Lemon Meringue Pie

When our son Drew was about 7 years old, I had a friend in her mid seventies named Henrietta, but she preferred to be called "Hank". We worked in the same department store. Hank only worked three half days a week so she could see people, learn the latest jokes and have lunch. Drew liked Miss Hank and one day we had lunch with her. When the waitress came to the table for the dessert order, Drew piped up with his request. "I'll have Lemon Low-Rang Pie please." Hank snickered at the time and said she'd have the same. She laughed out loud when she related the story to some mutual friends a bit later. I can't make this pie without smiling just a bit, remembering Drew ordering his dessert.

1 Cup sugar
5 Tablespoons cornstarch
1/8 teaspoon salt
2 Cups boiling water
3 eggs, separated
1 Tablespoon butter
4 Tablespoons fresh lemon juice
2 teaspoons lemon zest
1/8 teaspoon salt
1 teaspoon warm water
1 Tablespoon sugar
¼ teaspoon lemon extract
1 baked 9-inch pie shell (pastry or crumb crust)

Mix first 3 ingredients; add boiling water and cook over very low heat until thick. Cover and cook an additional 8 minutes over the lowest possible heat. Don't peek until time is up. Then the mixture should be clean and transparent. Beat egg yolks and pour in a little of the hot mixture to temper the yolks. Do this a couple more times. Pour the tempered egg mixture into the hot mixture and cook 1 minute stirring constantly. Remove from the heat; mix in the butter, lemon juice and zest. Cool.

Add 1/8 teaspoon of salt and the warm water to the egg whites. Beat with rotary mixer until just stiff. Add the extract and 1 Tablespoon of sugar. Continue beating until very stiff. Pour filling into pie shell, top with meringue, and bake at 300 degrees for about 15 minutes or until light brown.

Funeral Pie

Funeral pie is really a two-crust raisin pie and was a dessert staple served in church halls after funerals, most often served in the middle of winter when fresh fruit was not available. Raisins were used because they held up as dried fruits and were relatively available. The pie also had a lot of flavor.

2 crusts for a 9-inch pie
1 Cup raisins
1 Cup water
½ Cup sugar
2 Tablespoons butter
2 Tablespoons all purpose flour
2 egg yolks
1 teaspoon lemon zest
3 Tablespoons fresh lemon juice

Preheat oven to 450 degrees. Line a 9 inch pie plate with pie pastry. In sauce pan bring the raisins and water to a boil. Add the sugar. Stir until the sugar is dissolved.

Remove a ½ cup of the mixture and chill quickly by placing in the freezer. Stir into the cooled mixture the butter and flour. Return the chilled mixture to the saucepan. Cook and stir over low heat until the flour thickens the mixture. Remove from the heat. Temper the egg yolk, lemon juice and zest with a small amount of the raisin mixture. Then stir into the sauce pan.

Pour filling into pastry. Moisten the rim of the pie crust with water. Cover the pie with a second crust. Press the edge down to seal and then crimp. Cut several vents into the top of the pie. Brush the top crust with cold milk and sprinkle with sugar. Bake at 450 for 10 minutes then reduce to 350 for 20 minutes.

Grandma Pickerell Cake

A neighbor of my parents shared this recipe from her grandmother, hence the cake's name. Where I grew up, walnuts were always black walnuts. This makes for a very strongly flavored cake. I usually use English Walnuts or Pecans for this cake. If you use black walnuts make sure you check closely for pieces of shell. The year my mother should have gotten reading glasses she made this cake. It was like eating something with bits of wood and nails laced through it. Yes, shortly after this disaster the reading glasses were a fact of life for mother.

½ Cup Wesson Oil (vegetable oil)
2 Cups sugar
2 eggs, well beaten
4 Cups peeled and chopped apples
2 Cups sifted flour
¾ teaspoon cinnamon
½ teaspoon allspice

½ teaspoon nutmeg
2 teaspoons baking soda
1 teaspoon salt
2 Cups chopped walnuts

Cream sugar and oil together until creamy and fluffy. Add egg gradually, beating well after each addition. Stir in chopped apples. Sift all dry ingredients. Stir into apple mixture by thirds. Blend in chopped nuts. It is best to use a wooden spoon after the creaming is done. This is a very thick batter. Bake in a greased and floured angel cake pan. Bake at 350 degrees for 1 hour. Cool thoroughly before removing from pan. Place on plate right side up.

Molasses Kisses

This recipe comes from my German grandmother, Clara Rose Fritz Emling. She was a very good cook and baker. Her only downfall in this part of homemaking was never giving any of her recipes with quite the right instructions, or omitting a crucial step or two. Maybe that was her way of protecting her culinary secrets, or maybe it was a way of testing the recipient of one of her prized recipes. This one works.

1 Cup sugar
2/3 Cup butter
2 eggs
2 Cups flour
1 Cup molasses
1 Cup strong coffee (cold)
1 teaspoon baking soda, dissolved in the coffee
1 teaspoon each of ginger, cinnamon and allspice

Cream the sugar, butter and eggs together. Add the spices, molasses and coffee. Slowly add the flour beating after each addition. Pour this thin batter into a jellyroll pan that has been greased and floured. Bake in a preheated 350 degree oven for 15 to 20 minutes.

Remove from oven and place on a cooling rack. While still warm glaze with a thin frosting combination of powdered sugar and milk. Start with a cup of confectioners sugar, 2 Tablespoons of milk, and a teaspoon of vanilla. Stir until smooth. Add additional milk until the icing drips from a spoon like an icicle hangs from a roof. Smooth over the top of the warm cake. Cool completely. Cut large squares and serve with vanilla ice cream. My father liked this cake best 2 or 3 days old with whole milk poured over the top of the dried cake.

Oatmeal Cake or Harvest Cake

My very favorite aunt had this recipe among her things when she passed away. Missing were the directions for assembling the cake and baking instructions. I managed to figure that part out. It reminds me of my Aunt Toni. She always looked her best in the colors of autumn and this cake smells like that season to me. Enjoy this any time of year with a big pot of tea made with loose tea. Eat the cake, sip the tea and when you are finished, tell each other's fortunes from the leaves in the bottom of the cup. That's just what my grandmother, Mary Seroy, would have done when her daughter, Toni made this dessert.

1 Cup Old Fashioned Oats
1¼ Cups hot water
½ Cup margarine
1 Cup brown sugar
1 Cup white sugar
2 eggs
½ teaspoon salt
1 teaspoon baking soda
½ teaspoon vanilla
1½ Cups all purpose flour

Mix the oats and hot water in a small bowl and let stand. Cream the sugar margarine together until light and fluffy. Add the eggs one at a time beating between additions. Stir in the oats and water then add the balance of ingredients. Pour batter into 9 x 13 inch pan baking pan that has been greased and floured. Bake at 350 degrees for about 40 minutes. Remove from oven when a toothpick is inserted into the middle of the cake comes out clean. Remove from oven and let cool on a rack for 5 minutes.

Icing for the Oatmeal Cake

3 Tablespoons melt butter
5 Tablespoons brown sugar
5 Tablespoons milk
1 Cup coconut
½ Cup chopped nuts

Mix all the icing ingredients together. Spread over the slightly cooled cake. Place under the broiler and broil until the mixture bubbles and browns. Watch carefully, it burns easily. If that happens, scrape off the top and do it again.

Pound Cake

This cake is great plain or the perfect platform for fruit or sauces. Many cakes take a whole grocery store to make, not this one.

1¼ Cups butter
2¾ Cups sugar
5 eggs
1 teaspoon vanilla
3 Cups all purpose flour
1 teaspoon baking powder
¼ teaspoon salt
1-10½ ounce can evaporated milk.

Preheat the oven to 350 degrees. Grease and flour a 12-cup bundt cake pan. Beat at low speed butter, sugar, eggs and vanilla in a large mixing bowl scraping bowl constantly for 1 minute. Beat at high speed, scraping constantly for 5 more minutes. Mix together all the dry ingredients. Beat in dry ingredients and milk adding alternately in thirds on low speed. When all ingredients are incorporated pour into the prepared pan. Bake 70 to 80 minutes until toothpick inserted comes out clean. Cool in pan on rack for 20 minutes; remove from pan and cool thoroughly.

Pineapple Upside Down Cake

This one is our friend Warner's favorite. Warner thought is would be extremely difficult to prepare since the pineapple rings and juice needs to be kept at the top of the cake. "Shhhhh don't tell him: actually it's easy to make, and the only trick is to flip it upside-down onto a serving platter when it's cooled."

For the bottom of cake
1 15-ounce can of pineapple rings
10 Maraschino cherries
½ Cup light brown sugar
2 Tablespoons butter

One egg cake
1¼ Cups all purpose flour
1 Cup sugar
1½ teaspoons baking powder
½ teaspoon salt
¾ Cup milk
1/3 Cup margarine
1 egg
1 teaspoon vanilla extract

Spray a 9 inch cake pan with vegetable spray. Set aside. Sift all the dry ingredients together into a bowl and set aside.

Cream the margarine and sugar until light and fluffy with an electric mixer. Beat in the egg and vanilla. Beat in dry ingredients and milk adding alternately in thirds at low speed. After all ingredients are incorporated beat for 3 minutes.

Drain the pineapple and cherries. Arrange in a 9 inch round pan with a cherry in the middle of each ring and others around the edge. Sprinkle the brown sugar over the top and dot with the butter. Pour cake batter over the arranged fruit.

Bake in a preheated 350 degree oven for 35 to 40 minutes until a toothpick inserted comes out clean. Cool completely on a rack.

Pumpkin Pie Dessert Squares

This is a great dessert to serve from October through December. You don't have to make a piecrust and it is easy to carry to a friend's house. Cut the servings as large or as small as you want. I got the recipe from my neighbor Jan, in Enid, Oklahoma.

1 Package Yellow Cake Mix
½ Cup butter or margarine, melted
1 egg
3 Cups (1 pound 14 ounce can) pumpkin pie mix
2 eggs
2/3 Cup milk
1 Cup reserved cake mix
¼ Cup sugar
1 teaspoon cinnamon
¼ Cup butter or margarine

Grease the bottom only of a 9x13 inch pan. Reserve 1 cup of cake mix for the topping. Combine remaining cake mix, butter and egg. Press into pan. Prepare filling by combining pumpkin pie mix, eggs and milk. Pour over the crust. For the topping combine the cup of reserved cake mix, ¼ cup sugar, cinnamon and ¼ cup butter. Sprinkle over the filling. Bake at 350 degrees for 45 to 50 minutes until a knife inserted near the center comes out clean. Serve with whipped topping.

If using 1 pound of solid-pack pumpkin, add 2 ½ teaspoons pumpkin pie spice and ½ cup packed brown sugar.

Pizzelles (Italian Dessert Cookies)

6 eggs, beaten
½ pound margarine, melted
1½ Cup sugar
3½ Cups all-purpose flour
4 teaspoons baking powder
2 Tablespoons (1 ounce) vanilla, almond or anise

Beat eggs, adding sugar gradually. Beat to smooth. Add cooled melted margarine and flavoring. Sift flour and baking powder and add to egg mixture   Dough will be sticky enough to be dropped by spoon.

Using an electric Pizzelle iron drop rounded teaspoonfuls for each cookie. Bake according to manufacture's instructions. Cool completely on a rack. Store in an airtight container.

Lemon or Orange Pizzelles

Use one ounce lemon or orange flavor in place of the vanilla. Add lemon zest for lemon or orange zest for the orange flavored cookies.

Chocolate Pizzelles

Add the following ingredients to those in the recipe above. Sift with flour and add to egg mixture.

½ Cup cocoa
½ sugar cup
½ teaspoon baking powder

Chocolate Rum Pizzelles

Use one ounce rum flavoring in place of the vanilla.

Snickerdoodles

Throughout the road show, at every assignment I was always deeply involved with the Officers Wives Club, even serving as president at one base. A beneficial volunteer organization, the OWC would be helping the military community in a variety of ways. From bake sales, to the thrift store, to helping younger families in countless ways, the OWC is a very active and effective organization. Frequently we would all bring something, and since desserts were one of my favorites, this recipe got used a lot.

As a child I referred to these as "cookies with nothing in them". They were a staple of many cookie jars in the 50's and 60's. This recipe uses cream of tartar. Prior to commercially made baking powder, baking soda in combination with cream of tartar was commonly used instead.

1½ Cups sugar
1 Cup margarine
2 eggs
2¾ Cups all purpose flour
2 teaspoons cream of tartar
1 teaspoon baking soda
¼ teaspoon salt
2 Tablespoons sugar
2 Tablespoons cinnamon

Preheat oven to 400 degrees. Mix 1½ Cups sugar, the margarine, and eggs. Stir in flour, cream of tartar, baking soda, and salt. Shape dough by rounded teaspoons into balls. Mix 2 Tablespoons sugar and the cinnamon; roll balls in mixture to coat. Place about 2 inches apart on ungreased cookie sheet. Bake until set, 8 to 10 minutes. Immediately remove from cookie sheet to a rack and cool completely.

New England Squash Pie

You can also use pumpkin or any winter squash for this recipe. Bake and puree first.

1¾ Cup strained mashed squash
1 teaspoon salt
1½ Cup milk
2 large eggs
1 Cup sugar
1 teaspoon cinnamon
½ teaspoon nutmeg
½ teaspoon ginger
1 Tablespoon melted butter
1 pie crust

Beat all of the above together with rotary beater. Pour into pastry lined pie pan. For a little more crispiness, have the bottom pastry a little thicker than 1/8 inch. Bake at 425 degrees for 45-55 minutes, or until a silver knife comes out clean. The center may still look soft, but will set later. Serve slightly warm or cold.

Chocolate Trifle

Your favorite brownie recipe
½ Cup Kahlua or other coffee flavored liqueur
3 3.9-ounce packages pudding - prepare according to package directions
1 12-ounce container frozen whipped topping - or 2 Cups whipping cream, whipped
6 1.4-ounce English toffee flavored candy bars, crushed

Prepare your brownie recipe (a mix works fine) and bake in a 9x13 inch pan. Prick top of warm brownies using a fork. Drizzle warm brownies with Kahlua. Let cool, crumble. Prepare pudding and let cool. Place 1/3 of crumbled brownies in bottom of a 3 quart glass bowl. Top with 1/3 of the pudding and 1/3 of the whipped topping and then 1/3 of the crushed candy bars. Repeat twice, ending with the crushed candy on top. Or set in individual dishes. Chill 8 hours.   Makes 16-18 servings

Cindy's favorite Brownies:
3 one-ounce squares of chocolate
1 Cup butter
2 Cups sugar
4 eggs
2 teaspoons vanilla
1½ Cups flour
1 teaspoon baking powder
1 teaspoon salt
1 Cup chopped nuts (optional)

Melt butter and chocolate. Beat the sugar into the warm mixture. Add the eggs, one at a time. Beating after each addition. Be sure to temper the eggs so they don't cook in the mixture. Add vanilla and dry ingredients mixing just until all is moistened. Pour into greased 9x13 inch pan. Bake at 350 degrees for 30 minutes

Unbaked Fruit Cake

*I think our son Drew wanted me to include this recipe in
case I get too old to send him fruitcakes every year. It's messy but
easy to make. There are no great secrets except to lightly dampen
your hands when pressing the mixture into the pans. If kept in the
refrigerator or freezer it will last nearly forever. If you ever visit
my friend Jenny in England, please bring her at least one cake.
Graham Crackers are something only purchased in specialty
stores in England and are very expensive as they are imported
from the States. I am not sure about the availability of
marshmallows. Jenny doles out this cake in fine slices to her
bridge grup. "Only when they are very good and I think they
deserve a special treat," Jenny said. So it's in the book for Jenny
and Drew.*

¾ Cup milk
1 pound large marshmallows
1 pound graham crackers
1 pound dates
1 Cup raisins
½ Cup currants
1 pound candied red cherries
1 pound candied pineapple
2 Cups walnuts
2 Cups pecans
Additional whole nuts and fruits for decoration

Cut waxed paper to line pans. This will make 6 pans that
are 2x3x5 inches. You only need one pan. After you press the
mixture into the pan to form it, it can be pulled out and the pan
relined for the next cake. It is advised to have two people working
together. Being elbow deep in this sticky stuff makes relining the
pans very difficult if doing it alone.

Cut or chop dates and fruits to be used in the cake. Chop
nuts coarsely. Crush graham crackers with a rolling pin between
waxed paper or in a food processor. In a very large pan or bowl,

182

coat the fruits and nuts with the graham cracker crumbs. Set aside. Scald milk in 4 or 5 quart saucepan over low heat. Add marshmallows. Stir constantly until the marshmallows "disappear" and there is only sticky foam left. Work quickly and pour mixture over the fruit and nut mixture. Stir with a wooden spoon until all dried parts are incorporated.

Press into lined pan. Make sure that the cake is pressed into the corners of the pan and that there are no air holes or voids. Remove the first cake and continue until there is no batter left. While the person pressing the loaves into shape rests and washes up, the helper can trim the excess paper off the cakes.

Decorate the cakes with slices of pineapple, nut halves and red or green cherries. Place cakes on a tray. Cover with a tea towel. The cakes will now cure or dry out for a week or so. After they seem firm to the touch and not sticky, wrap in plastic wrap and then wrap in foil. Make sure the shiny side faces out. Keep in a cool place, refrigerator or freezer. The nuts are the only ingredients that will actually spoil. After a month or so, they can become rancid if not kept cool.

<u>Vanilla Pudding (Blanc Mange)</u>

This recipe comes from my Home Economics course in high school. It can also be called Cornstarch Pudding. I prefer the name Blanc Mange, it just sounds better. Have it plain, use it in other recipes, add fruit or make the Brandied Peach Dessert. It's simple and very inexpensive. It is best when made with whole milk. Skimmed milk just does not work. Period.

3 Tablespoons cornstarch
¼ Cup sugar
1/8 teaspoon salt
2 Cups milk
1 Tablespoon butter
½ teaspoon vanilla

Mix cornstarch, sugar and salt together in a 1 quart saucepan. Add about ¼ Cup of the milk to the dry ingredients. Stir until smooth. Add the rest of the milk. Cook over medium heat stirring constantly until thickened. Cook one minute after it begins to bubble. Remove from heat. Stir in butter and vanilla. Stir constantly while cooking. This will eliminate scorched spots and burning. Pour into a bowl to cool. Cover with plastic wrap to eliminate a skin from forming.

Marti's English Toffee

1½ Cups finely chopped pecans
1 Cup very cold butter
1 Cup sugar
1 Tablespoon vanilla
¾ to 1 Cup semi-sweet chocolate chips

Have all ingredients ready when you start. When the toffee gets to the right color, every thing moves very quickly. Remember this stuff is really, really hot.

In a heavy skillet on high heat, stir absolutely constantly the butter and sugar until a caramel forms and is the color of "Heath Bars." Add the vanilla, standing back; it will spatter. Pour in 1 cup of nuts and stir. Pour immediately onto a marble slab or heavy cookie sheet. While still quit hot, sprinkle the chocolate chips on the candy. As they melt spread the chocolate evenly over the toffee like a frosting. Dust with nut bits. Cool thoroughly. I use the back porch during winter months. Break into pieces. Keep in an air tight container.

For the Chocolate Trifle: break half of the toffee into tiny pieces. Use a knife to chunk it up. Makes about 1 pound.

After Thoughts

I have threatened to write some sort of cookbook for a very long time. If it wasn't for my friend Penelope marrying Scott, I don't know if I would have ever gotten around to writing this book. Promising her a cookbook as a shower gift put a bit of pressure on me to continue. Of course, Tony taking a photo of every meal we ate for months also kept me going. "If we're cookin', we're taking pictures!" almost became a daily battle cry. I thank them for giving me that little push.

I don't know how many rewrites we did, but the final version entailed the editing assistance of our focus group who gave us a lot of good input and assistance in catching all those persistent typos. Special thanks go out to: Ed and Suzi, Cindy and Warner, Sue, Erin, Memrie, Dent, Nelson, Larry, Bill and Linda, Carolyn, Evelyn, Nestor, Vicki, Joanie, and Nancy.

Now, take a second to think about all those cooks on television or who have written big books that are encyclopedias of food. Do you think they have ever had disasters? For the writer of this little book there have been more than a few. I had the smoke alarms activate on more than one occasion at home. I have made frosting that was so hard that it had to be sawed through to get to the angel food cake inside (hermetically sealed). My sister, Michele, probably remembers pounds of onions cooking all night long with 8 pounds of black-eyed peas for New Years Day (they got a little soft). Of course that was right after I burned cheesecake batter on the bottom of the oven the previous evening (the smoke cleared in an hour).

Or the time I blew up the stove with dinner inside: Tony still gained 20 pounds that year. I fondly remember another disaster with Tony's dog Scamp trying to get past me to the roast sliding across the floor. For years, I have tried to make fudge from cocoa, sugar and milk, ninety percent of my tries were harder than mortar -- I now make fudge using the Marshmallow Fluff recipe. Then there were times that I dumped too much salt or pepper into something. Sometimes it's just bad luck, like when the dry cured ham had gone bad and really stunk up the house (we did eat out that night). Just remember that cooking is art with science, not just science. Great portrait artists started out drawing stick figures.

There are some family recipes and techniques that should never be passed along: Doris' pancakes (stiffer than Frisbees), Lorraine's ketchup and bologna sandwiches (almost as good as a plain ketchup sandwich), Drew's 3400 degree pasta water (includes melted pan), Jim's diabetic pumpkin pie (not actually his, and he did not care for it -- He was just too polite to say anything when I forgot to add the sugar), hermetically sealed angel food cake (happens when you mis-read the thermometer), and my kidney stew with dumplings (which is a rare olfactory treat that permeates the entire house). Of course we immortalize those we love by telling the tales about them.

Try the recipes and make changes to suit yourself and your family. Cooking can be therapy. There can be just as much comfort found in cooking the food as in eating it. If you're adventurous, cook with your significant other as a team: just have an agreement about who's in charge, and when.

Best wishes,

Marti

Index

188

<u>Order Form</u>

Give the Gift of Extraordinary Cuisine
To Your Loved Ones, Friends, and Colleagues

CHECK YOUR LEADING BOOKSTORE OR ORDER HERE

☐   Yes, I want _____ copies of *Beans, Bullets, and Canapés* – at $16.95 each, plus $3 shipping per book (GA residents please add $0.85 sales tax per book). Canadian orders must be accompanied by a postal money order in U.S. funds. Allow two weeks for delivery. Quantity discounts available.

My check or money order for $_____ is enclosed.

Please charge my :   ☐   **VISA**   ☐   **Mastercard**

Name: _____

Organization: _____

Address: _____

City/State/Zip: _____

Phone: _____ Email: _____

Card # _____ Exp Date _____

Signature _____

Please make your check or money order payable to:

Marti Giacobe
7184 Hartman Road
Murrayville GA 30564
<u>**www.beansbullets.com**</u>

′
4
770-425-6735

Email: cookbook@giacobe.net
Online orders at www.giacobe.net
Or www.beansbullets.com

191

<u>Order Form</u>

Give the Gift of Extraordinary Cuisine
To Your Loved Ones, Friends, and Colleagues

CHECK YOUR LEADING BOOKSTORE OR ORDER HERE

☐   Yes, I want _____ copies of *Beans, Bullets, and Canapés* – at $16.95 each, plus $3 shipping per book (GA residents please add $0.85 sales tax per book). Canadian orders must be accompanied by a postal money order in U.S. funds. Allow two weeks for delivery. Quantity discounts available.

My check or money order for $_____ is enclosed.

Please charge my :   ☐   **VISA**   ☐   Mastercard

Name: _____

Organization: _____

Address: _____

City/State/Zip: _____

Phone: _____ Email: _____

Card # _____ Exp Date _____

Signature _____

Please make your check or money order payable to:

Marti Giacobe
7184 Hartman Road
Murrayville GA 30564
<u>www.beansbullets.com</u>

770-425-6735

Email: cookbook@giacobe.net
Online orders at www.giacobe.net
Or www.beansbullets.com

192